IN MEMORIAM – לע'נ
MOTTI

COPYRIGHT PAGE

Copyright © 2016 by

All rights reserved. This book or any portion thereof may not be reproduced or used in any manner whatsoever without the express written permission of the publisher except for the use of brief quotations in a book review.

Printed in the United States of America

First Printing, 2016

ISBN-13: 978-0692491515 (Custom)
ISBN-10: 0692491511

David Harp Publishers
30500 NW Hwy., Ste 410
Farmington Hills, MI 48334
www.davidharppublishers.com

Exclusively distributed by SKG Distributors - Brooklyn, New York
347-833-9057
solsbooks@gmail.com

Other Books by Author:
0 to 5760 in 60 Minutes (Jewish History), Spirit Press, 2006
God is Great; Setting the Record Straight, DHP, 2014
101 Magnificent Torah Sermons, DHP, 2015

Other Books by Publisher:
Pearls of a Patriarch; and Psychotherapeutic Anecdotes, DHP, 2015

All book are available for purchase at www.amazon.com or at www.davidharppublishers.com.

הסכמת ר' שמואל אייראנס, ראש כולל אברכים, דעטרויט, מישיגן

(Rabbi Irons' English translation of same may be found on the back cover)

יום ד' לסדר "ולמען תספר שמי בכל הארץ" תשע'ו

שלמא רבא יסגי להאי גברא יקירא המהולל בתשבחות איש האשכולות הר' שניאור זלמן פולטר שליטא.

נהנתי מאד מן הדברים שחדשת ולקטת: "ווערטלאך", גמטריאות, מעשיות (ספורים) ודברים הראוין והגונים להגיד בצוותא בין ידידים ובין אנשים הצמאים לדברי תוי'ש.

ספרך הנקרא "תבלין" הוא כמו קופת הרוכלים וקופה של בשמים: הם דברים שנותנים "תבלין" וריח ניחוח לחיינו ומתיקות לעבודתנו.

יהי רצון שיפוצו מעינותך חוצה ושתזכה להפיץ עוד מתורתך ולזכות את אחינו בני ישראל ותתן עוד "תבלין" לחייהם.

SECTION TABLE OF CONTENTS

Acknowledgements xiii

Introduction xv

How to read this book xix

Section I(a) 1

Section I(b) 61

Section I(c) - פרקי אבות (Ethics of the Fathers) 81

Section I(d) 91

Section II(a) 103

Section II(b) 119

Section III(a) 129

Section III(b) 171

Section III(c) 187

Jewish/Israel Trivia Module 201

ANECDOTES, VIGNETTES, LESSONS & STORIES
TABLE OF CONTENTS

Section I(a)

1. בראשית פסוק א
2. בראשית – נעשה אדם
3. בראשית – לזאת יקרא אשה
4. בראשית – קין והבל
5. בראשית – אישי/שמות התנך
6. נח – שמות ילדיו
7. נח – ומשה (דמיונות)
8. לך לך – גילי אברהם ונח
9. ויצא – גלעד
10. ויצא – מחנים (מספר הפסוקים)
11. וישלח – ויחץ הילדים
12. וישב – יוסף
13. ויגש – ובני דן חשים
14. ויחי – גורן האטד
15. שמות – ויאנחו בנ״י
16. שמות – בני בכרי ישראל
17. בא – החדש הזה לכם
18. בא – ולמען ספר שמי בכל הארץ
19. בשלח – אז ישיר
20. יתרו – וישמע יתרו (בעה״ט)
21. יתרו – (משה) הדבר הקשה יביאון
22. יתרו – הגבל את ההר
23. יתרו – לוחות
24. יתרו – כבד
25. תצוה – משה חסר

26.	אחרי – בקרבתם (לפני ה')
27.	קדושים – ואיש אשר יקח את אחותו
28.	נשא – יזיר עצמו מן היין
29.	בהעלתך – ויהי העם כמתאננים
30.	שלח – לך אנשים ויתרו
31.	שלח – עלה נעלה
32.	חקת – נחש נחשת
33.	בלק – לקב
34.	בלק – הן עם לבדד ישכן
35.	בלק – דרך כוכב מיעקב
36.	וגם בלק הלך לדרכו
37.	פנחס – זמרי בן סלוא
38.	מטות – ראובן גד וחצי מנשה
39.	פנחס/מטות – בנות צלפחד
40.	שופטים – בנה בית, נטע כרם, ארש אשה (לפי הרמב"ם)
41.	שופטים – עגלה ערופה
42.	תצא – בן סורר ומורה
43.	תצא – יבם
44.	תבוא – ושמת בטנא
45.	תבוא – תוכחה
46.	נצבים – ר"ה
47.	נצבים – וחיית ורבית
48.	וילך – לא אוכל עוד לצאת ולבוא
49.	האזינו – יערף כמטר

Section I(b)

50.	שבת
51.	שבת
52.	תשרי
53.	ער"ה
54.	ערוב תבשילין
55.	יו"כ
56.	יזכור

57. יזכור
58. סוכות – פרי עץ הדר
59. הלל
60. הושע'ר
61. פורים
62. פסח – והיא שעמדה
63. שבועות
64. שבועות
65. שבועות
66. שבועות
67. תשעה באב – חזון

Section I(c) - **פרקי אבות** (Ethics of the Fathers)

68. פ'א מ'א
69. פ'א מ'ב
70. פ'ג מ'ב, ג', ו'
71. פ'ג מ'יג
72. פ'ד מ'יג
73. פ'ד מ'כב
74. פ'ה מ'ה
75. פ'ה מ'ו
76. פ'ה מכ'א
77. פ'ו, מ'ג

Section I(d)

78. ארמ'ע
79. ויחי
80. טומאה
81. יחר
82. יעקב – אליהו
83. כי הם חיינו

84. מז'ט
85. נסיון
86. ממשה עד משה
87. מנין – רמז
88. נך – קרי כתיב
89. עצו עצה
90. שבע מצוות דרבנן
91. תהילים

Section II(a)

92. בראשית – ויהי מקץ ימים ויבא קין (כ'י בשם הראם והצרור המור)
93. בראשית – שעטנז
94. לך לך – אמרי נא אחתי את
95. וירא – משחיתים אנחנו
96. ויצא – טוב תתי
97. וישלח – מעבר יבק
98. מקץ – ראובן ויהודה
99. ויחי – ישימך
100. בשלח – בחר לנו אנשים
101. יתרו – נעשה ונשמע
102. שמיני – גחון
103. שמיני – שרץ מטמא
104. אמר – אלה מועדי
105. תצא – פי שנים
106. תבוא
107. נצבים – ר'ה

Section II(b)

108. אלקי עד שלא נוצרתי
109. החותך חיים לכל חי
110. ים של שלמה
111. ירמי' הנביא

112. כי היינו
113. משל אדיר
114. שכל ומזל
115. שם הוי'
116. תומכי תמימים

Section III(a) – Stories (ספורים)

117. אנעים זמירות
118. בחירות בארץ
119. בטוח חיים
120. בין אדם לחבירו
121. בעל התניא – שמואל מונקס
122. בעל התניא – שמואל מונקס
123. אהרן בעלזא הק'
124. גאון מווילנא
125. הגאון מרגצוב
126. דקדוק
127. וויכנין, דוד ז"ל
128. הקבה מדבר מתוך גרוננו
129. השגת גבול
130. התקשרות (רבי-חסיד)
131. ואחות לוטן תמנע
132. חזון איש
133. החידא
134. חפץ חיים
135. טרחא דצבורא
136. כל יהודי פנינה
137. לוי' של הריי"צ מלובאוויץ
138. לקוטי תורה
139. מגיד ממעזריטש
140. מזבוז ברוך
141. מיהו יהודי
142. משיח

143. סבי רי"פ
144. סיום מסכת סוכה עם הרבי מלובאוויץ
145. סלובייציק, רי"ד
146. עניוות ומענשליכקייט עם הרבי
147. שלום בית
148. שמירת שבת
149. שרײם בחב"ד
150. תוסיו"ט
151. תניא כ"ו
152. תחנון עם הרבי הריי"ץ בישיבת תו"ת ווין עסטרייך

Section III(b) – Stories (**ספורים**) cont'd

153. בעש"ט – מעין עוה"ב
154. בעש"ט – קדו"ה
155. בעש"ט – קפיה"ד
156. בעש"ט – תולדות י"י

Section III(c) – Mixed Bag

157. Baseball Rebbe
158. Dates
159. Dylan, Bob, שופר
160. Etymology
161. Israel Survival
162. Koufax, Sandy 1965 WS
163. Jury in Judaism – USSC
164. Munich Olympics, 1972
165. Symbols (sources)

---

166. Last one, משיח

ACKNOWLEDGEMENTS:

I owe a great debt of gratitude to several key individuals who, in one or way or another, have been extremely instrumental, invaluable and indispensable in, and have greatly contributed to, the publishing of this book, and in enhancing same.

First, a great big thank you goes out to my "phenomenal" interior layout & design artist, Atritex, from Upwork.com, (formerly Elance.com), as well as my "outstanding" cover design artist, PCL Design, Brooklyn, New York.

I'd also like to thank Rabbis Nachman and Baruch Levine, Rabbi Simcha Klein, Rabbi Yehuda Amsel, Rabbi Yehoshua Werner, Rabbi Dovid Polter (brother), Rabbi Levi Gordon and Moshe Heber, for all their wonderful *shiurim* and inspiring *divrei Torah*, thoughts, ideas, encouragement and anecdotal pedagogy. Each is very special, and I hold each very near and dear.

I'd be remiss if I did not make mention of my dear friend Levi Serebryanski.

Finally, I owe a debt of gratitude to my wonderful children, יוסף משה, מענדל, לאה. Not only are they ב'ה terrific children, but they further appreciate their father's short thoughts and anecdotes contained in this book (that I usually share with them fresh off the 'mind' press), and (at least most of the time) voice their pleasure thereto. They are a valuable sounding board, especially my בכור שורו הדר לו – יוסף, who constantly challenges me on my ווערטלעך, and makes certain that they are iron-clad and air-tight and that no gaps exist within them – he's done a fine job;

יישר כחכם!!

INTRODUCTION

The title tells the story of this book and its basic theme and thrust: T.A.V.L.I.N. (**T**orah **A**necdotes, **V**ignettes, **L**essons and **In**spiration). As it turns out though, this is not merely a random acronym, but rather the word/term תבלין (TAVLIN) happens to be the Hebrew word or term for "spice", which in common Hebrew vernacular refers to exactly this type of book and its contents (תורה תבלין).

It is mostly a collection of my own תבלין (TAVLIN); however, it is also interspersed with wonderfully unique and not very well known stories (סיפורי חסידים וצדיקים) – It is a collection of Torah (or quasi-Torah) stuff that I've amassed, collected, compiled and invented over a period of more than twenty years. The best way to describe this work is with a Yiddish term: ווערטלעך.

(As an aside, it must be said that though the consensus was to spell תבלין in English the way it is in fact spelled herein, with an "A", there is a reasonable position to spell it with an "O" as well, as in TOVLIN. Nonetheless, preferring to be true to form, I did not deviate, and spelled it with an "A". Yet, there's an important "O" acronym here as well: **O**bservations". For there is herein also a fair share of short ideas that are much better termed "observations", where you'll be fascinated by the idea(s) as mere observations – things that make you go "Hmmmm, that's interesting!")

As I said earlier, most of these חידושי תורה are in fact my own. Those that are not, I have clearly so indicated and have given due credit to the one(s) entitled to same; there are even a couple

xv

by my dear and beloved son Mendel, for whose Bar Mitzvah this book was first published (as a תשורה או מזכרת) in January, 2016.

The Stories' Section is of course just that: Stories. Though they're not *my* stories per se, they are favorites of mine because they are stories that speak to me; they speak to the depth of my heart, and are true favorites of mine. Most of them are not miracle stories. There is even a famous expression by a Chabad Rebbe who constantly maintained that ביי אונז מופתים וואלגערן זיך אונטער די בענקל (By us, Rebbes, miracles frolic underneath our chairs; they're so easy and they're so no big deal). No, these are stories of true introspection and wonderment and usually possess a מוסר השכל as well. Also, these are stories that, so far as I know, are not very popular or have not been well disseminated. (I've had to pick and pluck these from a multitude of sources over nearly twenty-five years).

I think and hope you'll find this book highly entertaining, engaging, and invigorating, and that you'll truly benefit greatly herefrom. I cannot say of any of my previous (or future) works that they were, or will be, "fun". This one (TAVLIN), however, is a "fun" book in the fullest definition of that word; *fun* to make, *fun* to write, and *fun* to publish.

All through this Book's compilation and writing, I have had opportunity to share glimpses of this Book's wonderful little treasures with friends and family, and they've truly *kvelled*, and luxuriated in, the original ideas, thoughts and stories contained herein. I'm certain you too will *kvell* and cavort in this cardinal colonnade of kosher codex-like chronicles.

In closing, I'm extremely interested in feedback of this Book. Please email me comments, questions, suggestions, (answers), and the like, to editor@davidharppublishers.com. I will address and or respond to your queries at my earliest possible opportunity.

With warmest regards,

Rabbi S. Polter, JD, MBA

HOW TO READ THIS BOOK

Because this book is somewhat unique in that although most snippets have Hebrew titles (because it just was more sensible to do it that way) the content is in English interspersed with Hebrew terms (as was necessary), I have broken it down so that you may easily locate, access, and enjoy this book in the best possible manner, as follows:

SECTION I contains four (4) subsections, as follows:

SECTION I – (a) are my personal חידושי תורה, organized chronologically by Torah portion, beginning with בראשית.

SECTION I – (b) are my personal חידושי תורה on מועדים, beginning with שבת (yes, considered a מועד), following a similar chronological order as above, with תשרי first, followed by ר"ה and so on, interspersed as well with other non-holiday, yet holiday-related, ideas, as they appear the very first time in the Jewish year (e.g. the prayer of הלל makes its first yearly appearance with the holiday of סוכות).

SECTION I – (c) are my personal חידושי תורה on פרקי אבות (Ethics of the Fathers).

SECTION I – (d) are my personal חידושי תורה on all other things, events, concepts, etc., organized alphabetically.

SECTION II contains two (2) subsections, as follows:

SECTION II – (a) are collected/compiled חידושי תורה (from other sources – with honorable mention) organized once again chronologically by weekly Torah portion.

SECTION II – (b) are collected/compiled חידושי תורה (not Torah-portion based) organized (thematically) alphabetically.

SECTION III (Stories Section) contains three (3) subsections, as follows:

SECTION III – (a) are collected/compiled stories organized (thematically) alphabetically.

SECTION III – (b) are collected/compiled stories of the בעש״ט only (my four favorites, from childhood)

SECTION III – (c) are several remaining collected/compiled stories that only lent themselves to English, not Hebrew, titles, organized, once again, alphabetically. This section also contains some other interesting items that did not make the cut or belong in any of the other categories. Don't miss the wonderful "Test your Jewish/Israel knowledge" trivia at the back of the book.

A FINAL NOTE: Though I have not formally indexed the items in pagination format (and trust me, there was a method to the madness), nonetheless, for extra easy access, I have numbered each item individually and have done so in "continuous" format, as opposed to renumbering each section anew. This, I felt, would cause less paging and quicker locating.

SECTION I – (a)
Torah Anecdotes - תבלין

בראשית ברא
מבני היקר (והבעל שמחה הב"מ) מנחם מענדל

The first פסוק in תורה (בראשית), that kicks off the "seven" days of creation, contains exactly "seven" words.

ADDENDUM:

As an extension to my dear son's wonderful insight, I have the following:

This פסוק as well contains twenty-eight (28) letters, the numeric equivalent of the Hebrew word כח (28). How fascinating is that? You see, this is clear and uncontroverted proof of, or most certainly a convincing רמז to, the first Rashi of the Torah (on this very פסוק).

Rashi writes: "Rabbi Yitzchak asks, why the Torah begins thusly – *In the beginning God created heavens and earth?* It ought to have begun with the first Mitzvah in the portion of בא, roughly 20% (or 14 portions) into the Torah? The answer," continues Rashi, "is that the Torah wished to make it very clear at the outset that first and foremost mankind must know and acknowledge that the world belongs to God and God alone, and that He giveth and He taketh, and that if He feels like taking land from one nation and gifting it to another, that's His call and it is final." (Rashi continues to make the argument for the right of the Jewish People to their Homeland – Israel).

Proof of this statement, says Rashi, is sourced in the following verse כח מעשיו הגיד לעמו לתת להם נחלת גוים (Psalms 111:6). כח = **28**

Also, the ר"ת of the first four words of that פסוק is המלך and מלכה. Indeed, this פסוק, it may be said, consummated the bond between the מלך (God) and the מלכה (His bride, the Jewish People).

Finally, "28" = "2" + "8" = "10". בעשרה מאמרות נברא העולם.

Notice too, that the word בראשית makes the words תשרי אב. This represents, in only the first word of תורה, the wonderful holy trinity of ישראל אוריתא קובה as follows: We know the word בראשית itself is בשביל ישראל שנקרא ראשית. The אב is the א-ב or אותיות התורה which refers to אוריתא. Finally, the month of תשרי represents the head or beginning or ראשית השנה which is first and foremost all about God, Creator (and creation) of the world (specifically the human), and God as father and king of the universe, the קוב'ה component.

בראשית – נעשה אדם בצלמנו כדמותינו

So one of the greatest mysteries, complexities and perplexities in all of Torah, upon which virtually all the commentary take and give pause, is found in the very first portion, בראשית.

Chapter 1, Verse 26 reads: ויאמר אלקים נעשה אדם בצלמנו כדמותנו... (and God said let **us** make man in **our** image and in **our** form). Of course the perplexity here is who's "us" and who's "our"? We all know that, at least according to Judaism (and even in large part according to most of the leading traditional religions, e.g. Christianity and Islam) God is the essence of "one", of perfect "unity", of the "singularity". What in the world is this sudden pluralism all about? And at the outset of creation (creation of man)? This verse, at least at first blush, appears extremely problematic.

This conundrum is further bolstered and highlighted by a similar pronoun problem several verses later.

Chapter 3, Verse 22 reads, ויאמר ה' אלקים הן היה כאחד ממנו (and God said, lo, man has become as one of 'us'). Really? Us? And though many a commentary (including רשי and אבן עזרא) offer their perspective, they still seem insufficient, and the problem still appears to persist.

Rashi writes...
> Although nobody per se assisted the Almighty in creation of man, nonetheless the verse is worded in such awkward prose only to teach us a lesson of humility and common decency. That is to say, that although God was and is the One and Only, nonetheless He consults with His *Palmalya Shel Maalah* (His Heavenly Court) for something as grand as the pinnacle of creation, the creation of man."

Rashi continues brilliantly, proving that this verse is clearly a lesson God wished to impart upon man:
> For if one takes a quick look at the immediately following verse (Genesis 1:27) one finds that when God actually creates man, not when He is contemplating or discussing it, He does it on His own without any assistance, even without the assistance of the *Pamalya Shel Maalah*. The entire verse is written in the singular, not plural, form. "...and God created man in *His* image, in *God's* image did *He* create man, male and female did *He* create them."

There are many more elucidations that shed a very bright light on an otherwise cumbersome verse. For example, Ibn Ezra has a fascinating grammatical thought on this verse. I highly urge my readers to retrieve your Genesis, preferably the *Mikra'ot Gedolot* version, which encompasses all the commentary I enumerated above.

Although Rambam (Maimonides) does not appear directly in the Pentateuch, you can easily find his erudition on this issue in his *Mishneh Torah, Sefer Ha'Mada, Hilchot Yesoday Ha'Torah* (the very first subject in the very first book of Rambam's fourteen book compendium), Chapter Four.

I'd like to propose the following original thought that I believe will address this dilemma quite satisfactorily.

Perhaps the vowelizer erred; or even if he didn't, there is most certainly room for a double entendre. That is to say, do not read נעשה אדם, but rather נ (the fourteenth letter of the Hebrew alphabet) עשה (made or created) אדם (man).

Thereafter, it is not to be read as בצלמנו כדמותנו (in *our* form, as *our* image), but rather as בצלם נ׳ and כדמות נ׳ (the Hebrew letters *Nun Vav* representing a greater and higher calling for man)[1]. The נ possesses the same meaning as the נ of נעשה – (I'll expound in a moment).

The ו represents the letter that is a direct channel and funnel from God to us, the conduit through which God feeds us with His perpetual kindness and sustenance. In Chassidic and Kabbalah lore, it represents the idea of *המשכה*, God's vent through which He is able to channel to us His light and countenance, the letter that represents prolonged expression. In other words, this entire concept is clear proof of, and really bolsters, the Kabbalic idea in that God created the world – and most importantly the human, ready-made with all he'll ever require to survive and thrive in the world – by initially installing the ו.

---

[1] At least partial proof of my theory may be found in two areas of תנך. First, פ׳ נצבים כט:יב where the Torah writes: כי את אשר ישנו פה עמנו.... Rashi himself is perplexed by the apparent superfluous nature of the word ישנו; it would have sufficed to merely write יש without נו. The two ultimately mean the very same thing ("there is"). Perhaps, however, my exegesis herein gives the selected word (ישנו) some oomph and meaning. Second is in מגלת אסתר wherein המן proposes to the king ישנו עם אחד מפזר ומפרד (there's one nation scattered throughout your lands). Here too it begs the question of why the need for the word ישנו; the word יש alone would suffice fine. But once again, with the above elucidation, this choice makes a lot more sense, and specifically as it applies to this story and the nefarious המן plot, as you shall see later on.

The נ represents one of two concepts or both (they are not in conflict). The letter *Nun* looks like this: נ . That is the figure of man. The letter has a protrusion on top, representing the head that overhangs the torso a bit. Then there's the straight line representing the remainder of the body, until you get down to the feet that again protrude, just as the bottom of the letter נ does. Therefore, נ was what and how, and the style and shape in which, man was made.

So it's not that God, as conventional wisdom goes, said "Let *us* create man in *our* image and in *our* figure…" Rather, what God said was, "נ shall create man in the image and figure of נ [with the ו built in, so that I may have a way in which to communicate or a channel through which to continuously breathe life into man and his universe (as God is constantly creating and re-creating)]," as more fully clarified above.

The second (or expanded) interpretation of the letter נ in this verse, in this context (and not in conflict with the first, and more applicable to נ of נעשה) is: נ enjoys a numeric value of 50. The number 50 has lots of meaning and importance in Jewish tradition. Haman's gallows which he would construct upon which to hang his arch nemesis Mordechai was, as fate would have it, fifty cubits in height.

The reason Haman chose to build a 50-cubit gallows, and not 40 or 30, is because Haman knew that 50, in Jewish lore, is the number beyond which fate and luck have no bearing or effect. He figured, therefore, it would be the appropriate height at which to construct the gallows, for certainly at that height the Jews are doomed. After all, thought he, the great attributes of God discussed in *Hassidut* and *Kabbalah* (kindness through kingdom) are seven. And even in its more esoteric and complex form, in its farthest reaches, it is 7x7=49. Thus, 50 that transcends all should be a safely superstitious number in which to execute his diabolical plan. Haman, however, once again made a fatal (literally) error. Indeed, he was correct in assuming that the number 50 is above all within the physical realm and that the Jews can't do anything or abstain from doing anything to achieve God's grace. Nonetheless, it's not a negative thing; it's a positive thing. 50 is the point beyond which God loves His people unconditionally, not contingent on doing or not doing anything. It's simply pure unadulterated love for the Jewish people. Therefore, no one messes with the number 50, not even Haman.

Applying this idea to our current paradigm, God created man with the נ because He loves His people unconditionally. As bad as we are and have been at times – and with all our negatives and shortcomings – He cannot forsake us. Why later on in the Book of Exodus when the Jews erect the golden calf, God tells Moses that He will eviscerate the Jewish people from the face of this earth, yet He does not. What stopped Him? The letter נ stopped Him. Not that נ is more powerful than the almighty Himself Who created it. But God had נ pre-installed to do the work of creation (in an abstract fashion, of course), so that regardless of what would happen He could not destroy man. For in the end, as the letter נ tells us, He loves us beyond any specific or isolated wrong. He might punish us for bad behavior as He's done previously on many occasions, but God will not and cannot completely do away with us.

Further proof of the above may be found in the Book of Numbers, Chapter 10, Verses 35-37, in the portion of *Be'ha'alotcha*. These two verses are set off by a mysterious reversed letter נ. The great commentary, Rashi, explains this oddity by stating that, "These two verses are good ones, positive ones. That which precedes and succeeds, however, is negative and speaks in regression of the Jewish people. Thus, these *Nuns* separate the good from the bad, the wheat from the chaff."

Here then we have a perfect example of what the letter נ is all about and what it represents. It's a letter in the quintessential חסד עליון (Higher Good), and therefore was chosen as *the* letter, out of the entire Hebrew alphabet, to parenthesize two awesome verses from that which comes before and after.

It is interesting to note that following נעשה אדם, the אדם becomes האדם, as in ויברא האדם (and He – God (alone) – created *the* man). האדם with the additional letter ה is the גימטריא of 50 or נ.

As an extension to the above, later on when man sins and God says (in disgust) הן האדם היה כאחד ממנו (man has become one of us), the difference between the words אדם and אחד is the מ and ח, which make up the word מח (brains or mental capacity; smarts). This tells us two crucial things: First, it takes the מח for the אדם to achieve or to reach the אחד (the wonderful and essential oneness of God). Second, only through this combination of אדם with אחד can man achieve or fully realize true and everlasting דעת, the very next word in that פסוק.

Finally, to help us better understand the ממנו reference (which is ostensibly problematic too, though we may have partially addressed it), through the חטא עה"ד man unfortunately made of אחד (almighty God) ממנו (many – gods).

בראשית – לזאת יִקָּרֵא אשה

We find that the very first formal thing named is אשה (woman). It is true that אדם predated his wife; however, at his birth, God doesn't formally or ceremonially name him. Rather, the תורה merely tells us that God created man (אדם). Even when discussing the animal kingdom, the תורה merely tells us that אדם named all the animals (חיות) accordingly, but doesn't go any further than that. When God creates the female (חוה) from the rib or thigh of man (אדם), however, He formally names the female species (אשה), the first of its kind in Torah.

This then is quite interesting, because as it turns out within the word אשה is hinted the three individuals in תורה whose names God changed. אשה is an acronym for אברהם, שרה, הושע. What's further interesting is that the first such name change, אברהם, references the very same terminology (יקרא).

Now of course your next question is, *how about* Jacob? *God changed his name as well, did He not?* Why then is he not included in this list?

I have four (4) answers to this question:

First, unlike the former three, where a letter was either removed or switched or added to the name, the latter, Jacob's, name was changed entirely (ישראל), not merely modified.

Second, unlike the former three, God Himself did not change Jacob's name, an angel did (at least at first).

Third, unlike the former three, we find something very odd about יעקב specifically in that his name change appears to have had little practical impact. We don't call יעקב ישראל; rather we continue to call יעקב יעקב, even after his name change, unlike all the others whom, once name changed, it sticks for the rest of their lives and beyond.

Fourth, יעקב is actually hinted as well within אשה in the final letter "ה" in two ways:
   a. The name ישראל contains "5" (or ה) letters;
   b. You'll notice once again that what's further unique about the יעקב name-change is that all other names (as above-written) either only a letter was added to the name, or a letter was changed (for example, שרי to שרה). In the case of יעקב, however, his name was completely changed (יעקב to ישראל). Nonetheless, one of his letters still remains the same, the י. The first modified letter in his name, though, is the second, from ע to ש. The distance between ע and ש is "5" or "ה", as in ע-פ-צ-ק-ר-ש (count the dashes, not the letters).

4

ויאמר קין אל הבל אחיו ויהי בהיותם בשדה ויקם קין אל הבל אחיו ויהרגהו ויאמר ה' אל קין אי הבל אחיך ויאמר לא ידעתי השמר אחי אנכי (בראשית ד:ח-ט)

These two verses have always eluded me. First, we have "ויאמר ויהי בהיותם קין אל הבל אחיו (and Cain said to his brother Abel) בשדה (and it was when they were in the field)....and Cain rose up and killed his brother Abel." What? What did Cain say to Abel? If he said something, shouldn't I know what was said? If he didn't, then of what purpose is it that Cain spoke to his brother Abel?

I think I may have found a modicum of pause, with the following re-interpretation of these verses:

ויאמר קין אל הבל אחיו does not mean "and Cain said to his brother Abel", for in truth he said nothing to him; he merely killed him. Rather Cain was speaking to himself. ויאמר קין (and Cain said to himself, underneath his breath in frustration and contempt) אל הבל אחיו, not meant as "to his brother Abel", but rather אל (merely by replacing vowels) may also mean "God". That is to say that Cain was bemoaning the fact that God only turned and paid all His attention to his brother Abel and not him. So he said in abject resignation, "Oh, I see, so He's the God of my brother Abel only!" What follows, of course, is cold-blooded murder. An important lesson for today's youth and the left in this Country. You remove God, murder follows.

Let's now attempt to decipher the following verse to make sense of it, as follows:

ויאמר ה' אל קין doesn't mean "And God said to Cain..." For if it did mean as we conventionally translate it, there was no need for the words אל קין (to Cain). Rather 'ויאמר ה followed by אי הבל אחיך would have been sufficient and would work just fine with the current simple interpretation: "And God said [obviously to Cain] where's your brother Abel?" Therefore, I think my interpretation fits better in that "God said to Cain [in response to his lament in the previous verse] no, you're wrong Cain. אל קין, I am in fact Cain's Lord, your Lord, too." This interpretation is further bolstered by the words in the verse that follow: אי הבל אחיך (where's your brother Abel?). These words ought to be interpreted as follows: אי is half the word אל, (or at least the ל is missing). In other words, God was telling Cain, "I'm only half your brother's; the other half I'm yours." And so thereafter, Abel responds לא ידעתי, as in "oops! Didn't know that, didn't realize that, my bad!" Proof of this interpretation can be found in the terminology used לא ידעתי which is usually past-tense (I did not know). If it were to be interpreted conventionally, it ought to have said לא יודע (the present-tense for) "I don't know". And what didn't Cain know? We get the answer in the final three words of the verse: השמר אחי אנכי (He who protects or guards – השמר, *the* Protector or Guardian of אחי (my brother), אנכי (protects me too)).

This second verse in the series is a further and perhaps greater lesson, twofold: First, remorse and regret is good. Second, you do the crime; you do the time, even after displaying a sense of remorsefulness, and even where one may be ignorant. Regret and remorsefulness alone do not and should not exonerate and absolve completely to the point of vindicating the crime committed or the punishment that follows, just like in the case of קין.

What is finally fascinating is that here we see how jealousy was the root cause of the first murder (and to make things worse, brother on brother). קין contains the root letters (שורש) of the Hebrew word for jealousy (קנאה). (If not perfectly, it is certainly a נוטריקון of sorts, or alliteration).

בראשית – אישי (שמות) התנך

I find it interesting that the names of קין children virtually mirror the names of his brother's שת children:

קינן	קין
חנוך	חנוך
ירד	עירד
מהללאל	מחויאל
מתושלח	מתושאל
למך	למך

THREE OBSERVATIONS REGARDING THE ABOVE

1. Now of course you're all saying to yourselves, *well of course, they're brothers, their children are cousins after all, stands to reason, you find no different today*. Well, this may be true; however, first, who were they naming after anyhow? The only reason you find today that cousins share names is because they're named after mom or dad's side, but that couldn't have been the case back then. Second, then why the subtle differences? If in fact these children were named after the same individuals, why the difference in version? Third, why out of all these names did only the name חנוך survive? (I have no answers).

2. Even more amazing is that the final descendant of קין (נעמה) married נח, which would then indicate that in fact the seed of קין, after seven generations, unlike conventional wisdom, was not wiped out. Perhaps then the קין curse (for the murder of his brother) only applied to male offspring.

3. Finally, a mysterious FYI. Just as Torah gives the age of למך בן קין when he gave birth to שת, so too the Torah gives us the age of the other למך (no קין connection). And eerily the ages are 77 and 777 respectively.

נח

It is very difficult to understand why the order of Noah's children is שם חם יפת when יפת was the בכור and thus logically should come first. רש״י explains that the Torah first mentions the righteous, thus the reason for starting with שם. But this is still unsatisfactory, for then why does חם follow? In order of righteousness, יפת ought to follow שם. Perhaps one may say that what happened here is that the Torah didn't wish to reorder everyone, merely switch places – שם for יפת because Torah only sought to move שם (the greatest of the sons) to the top of the heap, and nothing more. This explanation, however, is still insufficient because חם was actually the youngest, thus he should have been placed last in any event. Perhaps we may answer this conundrum by saying that just as in the הגדה we place the רשע near the חכם, so that the latter rub off on the former, so too in our case (שם to rub off on חם). This, however, is still insufficient as at the time of mention (birth), חם was not yet a רשע, only later on in life did he so become. Perhaps, therefore, we may say that just as נח father, למך, called him נח at birth because (בעתיד) זה ינחמנו (he will comfort us in the future), so too here the Torah already places חם in the הגדה position of רשע. (See also רמבן פ׳ו פ׳י).

נח ומשה

Only two places in all of Torah do we find the verbiage ותמלא הארץ אותם: In נח for bad, in that crime flooded the earth, and in שמות, discussing the rapid birth rate of the Jewish people while enslaved in Egypt.

I think we may postulate that which many great historians (e.g. Mark Twain, Paul Johnson) have already maintained and proven long ago, that the Jews even out the world, that we contribute perfect equilibrium, that we level the scales.

The first ותמלא הארץ was in חמס (crime or loot). This began the grand moral degradation of society and ultimately served as impetus for the Flood and destruction of the world. After that point, it's not like the world got significantly better. Only after the Jews came around and began to populate the world anew ותמלא הארץ אותם (the very same words that first destroyed the world) – perfect symmetry – did the world and society at large finally come full circle and balance was once again restored.

My dear friend and mentor, Rabbi N Levine, posits that it goes even deeper than that, that the similarities are even more striking than you and I know, as follows: Here (in שמות) too, says the good Rabbi, we have an ark on water – Baby Moses in his little floating bassinet. And here too we needed Moses to come around and level that negative water (and Ark) from the days of נח. And Rabbi Levine points further to the Great מהרל who writes that there's a clear nexus between the 120 years it took נח to build the תיבה and the 120 years of משה life.

My good friend ר לוי סערעבריאנסקי adds further that there's even a greater similarity between the two stories/personalities as follows: Just as נח wished to exit the Ark to worship God and offer sacrifices, so too with משה רבינו. See אלקינו לה' נלכה ונזבחה. (See also *Back to the Sources* by Mr. Barry Holtz, JTS, Pg. 51)

לך לך
אברהם היה נח (58) כשסבו נח מת

ויצא – גלעד

Here we find something quite fascinating. ויצא is really the first sojourn for יעקב outside of Israel. It turns out to be a very long and tiring journey. He finally reaches the city of גלעד after 22 years of exile; that's his last stop in the diaspora before he returns to his homeland (to *our* homeland). There he makes a pact with his father-in-law לבן. In other words, we've come full circle. ויצא בגימטריא גלעד.

Furthermore, לבן as well hints to the same type acknowledgement. He calls upon אלקי אברהם ואלקי נחור. Why? I understand why not אלקי יצחק (probably not too fond of his brother-in-law), and I understand why not אלקי יעקב (not too fond of his son-in-law either). But why אברהם and נחור?

I think the answer is that indeed לבן as well had an epiphany and subtly related same in this expression. How so? Well we begin the פרשה with ויצא יעקב מבאר שבע וילך חרנה. The term חר(נ)ה is אותיות (ה)חרן. The term אלקי נחור is אותיות מבאר אלקי אברהם. In other words לבן himself acknowledges that יעקב has been through enough and has suffered significantly at his and עשוs hands and it's time to return to whence he came.

Finally, indeed when יעקב departed באר שבע he left אלקי אברם (not in actuality, but figuratively). In other words, once one leaves the holy confines (אדמת קודש) of ארץ ישראל and enters חרן (a euphemism for גלות – like Rashi says: חרן מל' חרון אף של עולם) one has indeed removed oneself from everything truly sacred (and has embarked on a journey toward אלקי נחור which by alliteration may transform into אלקי נכר (a strange god, not the One True Lord)).

ויצא

FYI, the final word of this portion (מחנים) possesses a numeric value of 148 or קמח, the very number of פסוקים in ויצא. I wonder why then is this not the selected word at the end of the פרשה, as is customary, to represent the number of פסוקים? It's certainly the most logical.

וישלח
(אפ' להגיד) פורים תורה
(אבל אני מעדיף פסח תורה)

Wherefrom do we have a רמז מן התורה that at the סדר פסח it is in fact proper to first perform יחץ and only thereafter it's the children's turn (וכאן הבן שואל)?

Because in פ' וישלח when discussing the encounter between יעקב ועשו the Torah says ויחץ את הילדים (and יעקב divided the children into groups – by the mother who bore each). From here we may clearly derive that first comes יחץ and only thereafter הילדים (the children).

וישב – יוסף

יוסף בגימטריא קנו which term generally maintains a double meaning[2]:

1. "Purchased" (as יוסף was in fact purchased by the ארחת ישמעאלים).

2. (He nonetheless never sold out, was never able to be truly bought, because…) יוסף entire מהות was his קנו, his Creator, God alone, and none other.

---

[2] Which definition one applies depends on vowelization.

ויגש – ובני דן חשים

This week's Torah portion discusses, among other things, the posterity of Jacob. The Torah enumerates each of the twelve *shevatim* (tribes) and their respective offspring. When mentioning Jacob's son דן, the Torah uses the word בני, children (plural), as it does for all the other tribes. However, דן had only one child, חשים. Why did the Torah find it necessary to describe this child, of whom there was only one, with the very same word it uses for all the other tribes' children, ובני (and the children, plural)?

There are four possible answers, as follows:

First, חשים is the name of Dan's only child. However, חשים, oddly enough, is a plural name. Singular would be חש. So one may explain the seemingly odd use of the plural by saying that although he had only one son, nonetheless this one son's name is such that grammatically it makes sense to use the plural form, ובני, as opposed to simply ובן.

Second, the word חשים actually means skilled or talented. And the message in this verse is that the children and all future posterity of Dan, not only the one son he actually fathered, will be skilled, will be talented. And we clearly see that to be the case. Why, the Great Judge Samson, שמשון הגבור, was from the tribe of דן. The brilliant architect and engineer of the משכן (Tabernacle), אהליאב בן אחיסמך, was also a descendent of Dan. And there were others too. So the plural use is very much in order because it includes all of Dan's future generations.

Third, חשים was hard of hearing. On the one hand we may say that due to this handicap he was a real load and burden on his father, as big a load and burden as several children, hence the plural term ובני. On the other hand, the נחת he brought his father, דן, was as great as that of several children too. For we know that חשים was so incensed with the chutzpah of his great-uncle עשו, who wanted to stop Jacob, his grandfather, from being buried in the cave of מכפלה, that he decapitated עשו right then and there, thus ending the terrible life of עשו and making some recompense for all the pain and trouble he'd caused יעקב.[3]

Fourth, and finally, and the greatest lesson of all, is this. You must interpret these three words differently. Each of these three words has a completely different meaning than that discussed above, than the simple and obvious one, as follows:

ובני may be translated as "and you shall build," from the root word בנין. דן literally means justice or judgment. חשים can mean rapid, from the root word חש. Thus the hidden message in this verse is that one shall be **quick** to **build**, to establish and maintain, **justice**, or a system of law and order.

ויחי – גורן האטד

For years the following tradition, or perhaps dichotomy of tradition, the perfect polar opposites of tradition, grabbed me

---

[3] A possible fourth (let's call it 3.5). In next week's פרשה of ויחי, when יעקב blesses his children (the Tribes), he blesses Tribe Dan as follows: יהי דן נחש עלי דרך שפיפון עלי ארח הנשך עקבי סוס ויפל רכבו אחור (Dan shall be as a snake...who bites the heel of the horse and whose rider falls backward). Perhaps this was a premonition, as we know יעקב prophesied throughout his lifetime and especially during the ברכת יעקב, that his grandson נחש בגימט׳ חשים would one day bite (figuratively) עשו ultimately slaying him, as immediately above in "Third".

rather odd: In Judaism the greatest respect or deference for something or someone great is evidenced by donning a cap or hat, whether in the synagogue or engaged in a ritual rite. Juxtapose this tradition with the gentiles. What is the first thing one ought to do when entering a church or court? Remove all head coverings. Think of a sporting event you've attended. What are you asked to do prior to the national anthem being intoned, and in reverence to it and our flag? Remove your cap; a bare head is optimal. How is this? Why is this? The exact opposite ritual for similar sacred performances?

I may have found an answer.

During our forefather Jacob's funeral procession, Rashi relates that in the city גורן האטד, Jacob's son, Joseph, then the viceroy of Egypt, removed his crown and placed it on his father's coffin. Joseph of course did so as a show of respect, honor and dignity toward his beloved father, in essence crowning or canonizing him. The Torah as well relates that not only did the Jews mourn Jacob, but so did the Egyptians, for he was a saint in their eyes as well. Therefore, the Egyptians must have misunderstood the removal of Joseph's crown, and taken it to mean the very opposite of its intent, that Joseph was not crowning his dad as much as he was removing the crown from his head at such a somber or serious or sacred moment. In other words, for the gentiles it was the "removal"; while for the Jews it was the "coronation".

The greatest proof hereto is that Rashi continues: Upon witnessing, what the Egyptians believed to be, a de-coronation by Joseph, the Egyptians followed suit and removed their hats as well and placed them on Jacob's coffin.

Thus, a possible source for today's respective traditions.

שמות – ויהי בימים הרבים ההם ויאנחו

The טללי אורות writes that the word רבים in this פסוק is a רמז to the four גליות we Jews have endured, as follows: רומי בבל יון מדי.

I believe I have found a much more appropriate ר"ת for a four-גלות remez, as follows: First, these are hinted, I believe, in a more fitting word "ויאנחו", because after all, the definition of this word is that they (the Jews) sighed (a sigh of pain and anguish from the horrible labor and awful conditions they suffered in Egypt). Far more fitting than merely רבים - many.

Now for the רמז in ר"ת form.

The לך לך – והנה אימה חשיכה גדולה in פסוק on the מדרש רבה writes, that this פסוק hints to the four גליות as well. אימה נופלת עליו זו בבל, חשיכה זו מדי, גדולה זו יון, נופלת זו אדום. This was obviously a premonition to אברהם about his children's future suffering.

The word ויאנחו is an acronym for אימה (בבל), חשיכה (מדי), נופלת (אדום). We're still, however, missing גדולה. After we subtract letters א, ח, נ from the word ויאנחו, as above, the remaining letters spell יון, which according to מ"ר is the גלות represented by the word גדולה. There you have it!

שמות – בני בכרי ישראל[4]

The above caption is the first term of endearment God uses to refer to his Chosen People. "My son, My primogenitor, Israel." Within the first word (בני) of this three-word term we find a hint that God's love toward His People goes beyond all realms of logic and reason; that even the greatest of sinners is included in this accolade-laden description.

בני ר'ת ירבעם בן נבט

Jerabam, the most evil king of Israel,

who, as we know, was

חוטא ומחטיא את הרבים (the worst possible Jew).

Yet, even he shall some day be absolved, for he too is "My son, My primogenitor, Israel."

בא
החדש הזה לכם

It is interesting to note that the (skip/reverse) acronym for the above-captioned words/heading – words/verse that launch the beginning of *halachic* Torah – is הלכה.

---

[4] וראה מדרש רבה והצ'צ עה'צ פ' יסף ה' לי בן אחר, וגם מאמר הראשון של הרבי הרמ'ש באתי לגני תשי'א.

בא – ולמען ספר שמי בכל הארץ

The noun form of the word ספר (to tell or recount) is ספור (story). The pronoun form of the word שמי (My name) is שמו (His (God's) name). These two words share a similar numeric value of "346". A ספור is perfect and complete when it regards or recounts שמו (His name), and aggrandizes Him, His People, His Torah.

בשלח אז ישיר
שמעו עמים ירגזון...אז נבהלו...אילי מואב

First, why the different terms of reaction for the various nations? (E.g. ירגזון או חיל או נבהלו או רעד או נמגו depending on whether we're referring to עמים או פלשת או אדום או מואב או כנען).

Second, why עמים as opposed to ישבי פלשת as opposed to אלופי אדום as opposed to אילי מואב as opposed to ישבי כנען?

Third, and finally, the order of the five distinct descriptions of fear, that will envelope the five distinct peoples or nations, is: Noun verb / Verb noun / Verb noun / Noun verb / Verb noun. Perplexing!

Some would answer this triple conundrum by saying that this is after all a poem and so *all is fair in love and poems*, or that specifically in poetic prose this type vernacular and lexicography is rather picture perfect. I'd venture to say, however, that in

Torah, if at all, these games are kept to a minimum, and so I don't believe such poetic panache is justified here. Second, even assuming this is the case; it does not address all three questions.

Though I don't have the panacea, I do have some thoughts that could potentially address part of the trifecta conundrum, as follows:

The two "noun/verb" sets share a common bond. ירגזון and רעד are nearly the same גימטריא, off by only "2". Whereas ירגזון is 276; רעד is 274. The difference of "2" is merely the distance from one to the other, because of פלשת and אדום in between.

Another thought is that אדום and אילי, neighboring words, are the very same גימטריא, both "51".

Lastly, but not at all very least: The גימטריא of בלק + בלעם is 274, the exact גימטריא of רעד. What this indicates then is that the רעידה that grabbed מואב, and not just מואב, but specifically אילי מואב, referring of course to בלק, the consummate מואבי, the *king* of מואב, was in fact his collaboration and collusion with his prophet בלעם. It was the fact that what they sought to cook up against the Jews came back to haunt them severely, in terms of not only not cursing the Jews four times, but blessing them as well. And not just any blessings, but parts of which we have even incorporated into our סדור, and another which as it turns out is the only reference to משיח in all of Torah. That is the ultimate רעידה that must have grabbed אילי מואב, the fact that they were the impetus for empowering and emboldening and aggrandizing the Jews and the Jewish cause.

יתרו – וישמע יתרו (בעל הטורים)

בעל הטורים on this פסוק is once again (like another one - פ' פנחס - later in this book) very difficult to comprehend, because his גימטריא is once again off kilter, it just doesn't add up. בעה"ט writes that וישמע יתרו כהן מדין חתן is the גימטריא of והנה קריעת הים ומלחמת עמלק.

First, I'm not sure why the need for this גימטריא in the first place. Second, why the stretch or very tight fit in order to achieve this גימטריא? Third, and most importantly, the גימטריא is off, by a lot. וישמע יתרו כהן מדין חתן adds up to 1679; whereas והנה קריעת הים ומלחמת עמלק adds up to only 1665 (a difference of "14"). Though I don't believe I'm in position to answer my first and second questions above, I may have arrived at some semi legitimate answer to Question Three, as follows:

Perhaps if we can rework the פסוק to read וישמע יתרו כהן מן חתן (and יתרו, the priest of "heresy", father-in-law to...) this could satisfy our mathematical problem here. By removing the יד from מדין we now have the reduction of "14", reducing the total number of 1679 to 1665. And this is not simply a way of making the numbers fit so as to make the בעל הטורים look good (he doesn't require that from me). Rather this makes perfect sense, because in fact יתרו pre-revelation, pre-epiphany, pre-conversion, was in fact a heretic, an atheist, a pagan. And what in fact was the impetus for his coming around and seeing the light and his ultimate transformation and conversion? It was as בעל הטורים writes: והנה קריעת הים ומלחמת עמלק. When he witnessed these fascinating miracles performed by the God of Israel, he was convinced. There was still, however, a process, as he wasn't instantly converted. Therefore, he then became

כהן מדין, at least no longer כהן מן (no longer the heretic, the pagan). Perhaps this is what בעל הטורים intended; it is certainly the only feasible explanation I can come up with to reconcile this mathematical faux pa.

יתרו/משה (שמות חי:כב-כו)

It is interesting to note the contrast between verses "22" and "26". In Verse "22", יתרו advises his son-in-law משה to appoint a cabinet that'll alleviate much of the pressure and stress weighted upon the shoulders of משה.

כל הדבר הגדל יביאו אליך וכל הדבר הקטן ישפטו הם suggests יתרו (all the 'big' things they [the Jews] shall bring to you, and all the small issues they shall judge themselves [or your underlings shall handle and adjudicate]). Then in Verse "26" when משה implements his father-in-law's advice, here's what he says, את הדבר הקשה יביאון אל משה וכל הדבר הקטן (…all the 'hard or difficult' things ye shall bring to משה, but all the lesser ones…)

(A separate question is why does משה refer to himself in the third person[5]?)

You clearly see the difference between the two: יתרו said "big", while משה said "hard" or "difficult". Why the difference in terminology? In actuality though it would appear יתרו has it right. After all, יתרו uses poetic or symmetrical prose: "big" vs. "small". Conversely, משה uses completely asymmetrical prose:

---

[5] Another good question I have no answer for is: Did משה really need יתרו for this advice? Was this advice really that brilliant that משה couldn't figure it out on his own? This was his father-in-law's great epiphany? Isn't this common sense?

"difficult" vs. "small". So the question is not merely why the difference between father-in-law and son-in-law, but actually one appears to have it righter than the other, and oddly enough the righter one appears to be יתרו, not משה(?).

I think a possible answer can be this: Grammatically of course יתרו is correct. However, משה, upon his repeating, saw something and therefore hinted at something much deeper than the simple intent as follows: משה saw and therefore hinted at the חורבן ביהמ'ק, the most "difficult" issue (or pill to swallow) for משה רבינו. Therefore, משה tells the Jewish People את הדבר הקשה (the most difficult thing), not like his father-in-law כל הדבר הגדל (the biggest things) – not only is a different adjective used here, but a different noun as well. יתרו says "all things"; whereas משה says, "the thing". What "thing"? The חורבן ביהמ'ק. How do I know this? Because the גימטריא of the word הקשה is 410, the number of years the first ביהמ'ק stood before it was destroyed and Jerusalem left in ruins (circa 400 BCE). Perhaps that's the reason משה speaks in the third person. He's trying to say, "I won't be around then, so you won't be able to come to me, but you will have the משה of your generation to whom you shall appeal in times of dire straits (whether it is עזרא or נחמיה or whomever) that'll ultimately save the day."

יתרו – הגבל את ההר

God commanded Moses to cordon off the Mountain (Mt. Sinai) to prepare it for the giving of the Torah. Interestingly, the term for "cordon", הגבל, bears a numeric value of "40", the very sum of days Moses resided atop the Mountain to study and then receive the Torah from God. (Forty is also the number of years the Jews spent in the desert). Furthermore, the word ההר (The Mountain) enjoys a numeric value of "210"; the number of years the Jews were oppressed and enslaved in Egypt. In essence, what this פסוק then is saying (the deeper or hidden meaning behind it) is that God commanded Moses, "Cordon off the Mountain for a forty-day period (either literally or figuratively, but all the same), and that (the ultimate gift of My Torah) will achieve countering the effects of the 210 years My People suffered the hell they did, and shall serve as compensation and as atonement for how far they've sullied themselves while in Egypt."

This is also why the word "ההר" is the one specifically selected to represent the full extent of this lesson. Because indeed a mountain is generally humanly insurmountable, and so in this case it is not meant to indicate only the physical mountain, but as well the metaphoric mountain, the one we all must overcome every now and then, certainly the one the Jews had to overcome following their Egyptian escapade, or should I say nightmare. But overcome the obstacle they did. And through that effort, they achieved the וקדשתו (to consecrate the Mountain, and in so doing, consecrate themselves and God's Great Name and Glory).

יתרו
Juxtaposition of עשה'ד

I think there's something very telling about the juxtaposition or symmetry of the לוחות or עשרת הדברות. I will try to outline my thoughts here; I think you will find these quite amusing.

אנכי   לא תרצח

This one's quite obvious. The single greatest determinant in predicting a murderer (specifically genocidal murderers, like Hitler, Stalin and Pol Pot) is clearly whether they knew, appreciated, understood and internalized אנכי (I am thy Lord). If not, all bets are off, and anything is possible and any murder justified. (See בראשית; Item "4" supra).

לא יהיה   לא תנאף

Not a very difficult one. לא יהיה, don't have any other gods; be faithful and loyal and pledge your fidelity and fealty to the One and Only. לא תנאף, don't cheat on your spouse (wife), don't have any others; be faithful and loyal and pledge your undying fidelity and fealty to your one and only.

לא תעשה   לא תגנב

This one is a more difficult one and is not so self-evident.

First, they're the only two that share similar acronyms: לת. Second, the Talmud says that גנבא אפום מחתרתא רחמנא קריה (a thief in the midst of his theft calls out to the lord that he be successful). The juxtaposition of these two tells us that, "in fact the thief should be advised," says God, "you ain't talking to me. Rather when you steal you're calling out to the פסל, to a god made of stone or wood or even 'green'; I want nothing to do with it."

Third, and finally, the question is posed: Why the need for both לא יהיה and לא תעשה? Aren't they in essence saying the same thing, addressing the same prohibition? How do they differ? Don't *have* any other gods; don't *make* any other gods. What's the practical difference between the two? It seems redundant. The fact, however, that it sits side-by-side with its neighbor לא תגנב clues us in to a unique observation, as follows: What God is saying here is, "First, לא יהיה (don't have)!" You may, however, cleverly retort, "Okay, I won't have any other *currently existing gods* before me, but who's to say that I may not *make one*?" Because in the first prohibition of לא יהיה, the tone is very neutral, and appears to apply to *currently-*

existing other gods only. Therefore, God continues with the third Commandment, לא תעשה (don't even *make* any others). The idea behind it all is that, *to God is the world and all that is in it*. What follows then from that is that any time one uses any item or material in this world to create or build or construct he is in essence using God's item or material. Therefore, if you misuse an item or material or if you misappropriate an item or material, you are in fact "stealing" from God. This is what לא תעשה teaches us, and it is highlighted by the fact that it is placed as it is, side-by-side with לא תגנב.

זכור את   לא תענה

First, לא תענה is all about "witness", bearing false witness. The מצוה of שבת is the only one of the Ten Commandments that falls into the category of מצוות referred to as עדות (witness). However, secondly, and more importantly, if you indeed remember the Sabbath to keep it holy, you're assured against bearing false witness. For שבת doesn't only fall into the category of עדות, rather the whole idea of שבת is that it is *the* עד (the consummate witness) to the bond between God and His People, the Jewish People, as we recite throughout the שבת liturgy and hymns.

כבד את   לא תחמד

If you truly respect your parents, you will covet nothing. Respect, in general, and especially of parents, is the first and most crucial step in training and disciplining oneself in the art of self-restraint and against envy and jealousy. The idea of "respecting one's space" or "respecting one's property" or "respecting one's dignity" is the single and foremost greatest trait in protecting against covets. And the better and quicker you learn and hone the art of "respect", with first respecting and honoring parents, the quicker and better you will learn the art of respecting others, their space, their property and their dignity.

יתרו – כבד

Many of the commentary explain that the 5th דברה (כבד את) closes out the God Chapter and begins the mankind chapter. Up until this point it was all about respecting God. With כבד we begin with respecting man (parents first and foremost). Furthermore, the commentary further write that when one respects his parents, he is respecting God as well, because all humans have three partners in creation: Mom, Dad and God. It is therefore fascinating to note that כבד posseses a numeric value of "26", the numeric value of שם הוי-ה (the Great Name of God, the Tetragrammaton).

תצוה – משה חסר

Let's begin by posing the $64,000 question. Why is תצוה the only Torah portion, since his birth in the portion of שמות, wherein Moshe is not mentioned even once? Roughly 39/40 portions, beginning with the 2nd Book of Moses, the Book of Exodus, contains some mention of Moshe. Yet this week's portion lacks any such mention. Why?

I know of five answers to this question. I will attempt to credit each of the contributing individuals who have lent their logic, intuition and brilliance to answering this conundrum.

First, and the most common response, is as follows: In next week's portion, תשא, God, following the ugliness of the Jews erecting the Golden Calf, wished to annihilate the Jewish people entirely, and even made an offer to Moshe, "It'll be you and I, Moshe; we will start anew with a new nation." Upon hearing these words, however, Moshe challenged God, and retorted, "No! You will not do such a thing, For if You do, 'erase me as well from the Book that You have written' [the Torah]." Because God loved Moshe so much, He in fact capitulated and spared the Jews. God, however, did take Moshe semi-seriously, and erased him from one portion of Torah, the portion of תצוה.

Though an interesting observation, the question immediately posed is: But why *this* week's portion? Why תצוה? The "first" answer explains (perhaps satisfactorily) why Moshe is omitted from *a* Torah portion, but why *this* Torah portion?

(Therefore, we have answers 2-5).

Second. The Vilna Gaon (הגרא) writes amazingly as follows: Because Moshe's יאהרצייט (death anniversary – Adar 7) always occurs in the week in which we read the portion of תצוה, therefore God deemed fit to remove him from this portion as a show of mourning and voidness, symbolic of great men passing and their lack of continued earthly existence.

Third, is that the Hebrew words for Moshe's famous quote in תשא (next week's portion), I reference above, "No! You will not do such a thing, for if you do, 'erase me as well from the Book that You have written'," are: מחני נא מספרך אשר כתבת. The word for "Book" is "מספרך", spelled with Hebrew letters: מ, ס, פ, ר, כ.

As many of you likely know, unlike the English alphabet, the Hebrew alphabet contains both spelling and numeric significance. In other words, the Hebrew alphabet serves a double purpose: letters and numbers. The numeric value of the final letter of that word, כ, possesses a numeric value of "20". This then means, that what Moshe threatened God with was, "If You are not to forgive Your people, erase me from Book 20". Book "20" meaning portion "20". Portion 20 is in fact this week's, תצוה. This exegesis also puts Moshe in a positive light, in that it was Moshe's wish to be omitted from this portion, and God acceded.

Fourth is from the Rebbe of Bobov. He explains, that even though God knew he had to make good on Moshe's threat in some form, He was still very reluctant to do so, because God's love for Moshe was unprecedented and boundless. He knew, however, that he had to at least do something about Moshe's so-called *Chutzpah*. So God determined to remove him from a Torah portion, but simultaneously God was conflicted as to which one, and so He simply adjourned it week after week. When He finally reached the end of the cycle from the portion in which the story occurred, *Tisa*, God had no choice but to act, and He did. Therefore, it is תצוה, this week's portion, the very portion preceding תשא, the very last possible portion God was able to remove Moshe from, in which there's no mention of Moshe.

Fifth is my very own. Moses' quote to God is this: "If you, God, eviscerate the Jewish people from the face of the Earth, then מחני נא מספרך אשר כתבת (erase me too from the Book You've written)". Let's, however, read this quote (verse) slightly differently. Do not read מחני נא מספרך אשר כתבת; rather, read מחני נא מספרך אשר – erase me from Your Book אשר, bearing a numeric value of 501. Likewise, *Tezaveh* bears the numeric value 501 (the only portion in Torah that bears a 501 value). So what in essence God did was to grant Moshe's wish. Moshe asked God מחני נא מספרך אשר. And God did so.

Now the question that must be posed is why then did Moshe wish to be erased specifically from this week's Torah portion, תצוה?

As fate would have it, every תצוה reading is accompanied by another Torah reading, the portion of זכור, which recounts the nefarious עמלק nation and the hardships it caused the

Jewish people throughout their sojourns in the desert for forty years. We read this portion this week because תצוה is always the portion that immediately precedes the holiday of Purim, and the highlight of Purim is of course the triumph of the Jewish people over nefarious Haman, a direct descendant of עמלק. Moshe wanted nothing to do with עמלק (both in the here and now, as well as in the metaphoric sense of what עמלק stands for or represents). Furthermore, Moshe wanted to send a very clear message to all future generations, that as to עמלק (which in some fashion we, the Jewish people, suffer from even nowadays) there is no negotiating or appeasing – only total eradication – and so he removed himself (from being mentioned in the same breath (or week) as *Amalek*).

It is interesting and wildly fascinating to note the following (a phenomenon that hammers home and solidifies this point): There's a very significant shared term/word with respect to עמלק (as read in זכור) and in the following portion, תשא, where Moshe beseeches (threatens) the Almighty to erase him from His Book (תצוה). It's the Hebrew term for "erase".

In זכור we have תמחה (with Hebrew letters: ת מ ח ה). In תשא, the term for the same meaning ("erase") is מחני (with Hebrew letters מ, ח, נ, י [6]). No doubt you are by now all aware that in Hebrew, unlike English, the Alphabet serves (a double function), not only as letters, but as numbers too.

The numeric value of the term תמחה (as written in זכור) is 453. The numeric value of the term מחני (as written in תשא) is 108. Are you ready? 453-108=345, the numeric value of the name/word *Moshe* (spelled מ, ש, ה).

---

[6] On an aside, we may posit that God reversed his threat of annihilation of the Jewish People upon Moshe's threat, מחני, because He felt that if He reversed so would Moshe reverse his מחני. If you reverse מחני, you get the word ינחם (he will console/comfort). Moshe indeed made good on this reversal, and not only ended up consoling and comforting the Jewish People, but God too.

What Moshe was in essence saying was: "Because זכור is read only after we have completed the entire תצוה reading, therefore, God, please erase me until your people, the Children of Israel, have eviscerated the name of עמלק." Thus, Moshe in fact is not to be found in this week's portion, תצוה.

The lesson of course for all of us is to utterly destroy עמלק and everything it represents, its vile and epicurean tenets, its ideology and sacrilegiosity, even present in some form today, thirty-five hundred years hence, just as Moshe did thirty-five hundred years ago, by removing himself from the only Torah portion since his birth.

In the same vein, it is interesting to note that Hashem Himself is also absent from another Book we read during this week as well, the Book of Esther. Perhaps there too Hashem's intent was to serve as role model to Moshe, following which Moshe was to serve as role model to His children.

אחרי
בקרבתם (לפני ה׳)

It is interesting to note that the word בקרבתם (when they, the sons of Aaron, came close, to God), contains the same letters as the word בקברתם (their demise and burial – the result of their unrequited (wanting to) cleave to God).

OBSERVATIONAL
פ' קדושים פ'כ פי'ז

"ואיש אשר יקח את אחותו בת אביו או בת אמו וראה את ערותה...חסד הוא ונכרתו (he who taketh his sister, daughter of his father or mother, and cohabitates with her, this is a kindness and he shall be slain (by Almighty God))". I need not tell you how odd and perplexing this verse is. חסד הוא? It's a kindness? This low-life has done a good thing to engage in downright incest?

Of course רשי and רמבן, as well as other commentary, are as well perplexed and attempt to give this verse some greater meaning and substance. For example, some say that חסד הוא in this context is לשון חרפה (vernacular for "shameful" or "utter disgust"), and of course they bring proofs thereto. However, it still remains somewhat unanswered or unanswerable. After all, if that is what the Torah meant or wished to say, why wouldn't it say it?

Though far from a complete response – it is even moderately weird and perhaps chilling – I shall give you some reference, though I'm not entirely sure myself what it means or symbolizes or whether it even answers our perplexity.

See פ' וירא פ'כ פי'ב וי'ג as follows: וגם אמנה אחתי בת אבי הוא אך לא בת אמי...ויהי כאשר...ואמר לה זה חסדך (and lo my sister, daughter of my father, though not daughter of my mother...and it will be...and he said to her this is your **kindness**).

I leave it to my brilliant readers to decode and determine whether there's in fact a nexus, and what that nexus may be.

נשא – יזיר עצמו מן היין

It is interesting to note, while simultaneously odd, that, among other things, the פסוק imposes a complete ban on grapes for the נזיר (monk). Why grapes and all grape extracts?

Rashi explains that the reason the פרשה נזיר immediately follows the פרשה סוטה is because once one sees or appreciates the fate of the סוטה, logic dictates יזיר עצמו מן היין (one should refrain from all wine, really a pseudonym for all alcohol). This makes sense. But why did Rashi not write יזיר עצמו מן ענבים (one should distance himself from all grape products), just like Torah wrote?

I think the answer may be found respectively as follows. Rashi is in fact correct. When one witnesses or experiences or appreciates the severity of the סוטה it is most ideal that he refrain from all alcohol consumption as a means of steering clear of any and all frolic and frivolity that may result therefrom and thus cause unbecoming behavior. Torah, however, wishes to go one further and provide a סיג, a fence, a backstop. Therefore Torah does not just outlaw wine or alcohol, but any and all grape substances so that one not develop a taste for the truly prohibited (a grape extract or wine). In other words, Rashi writes the way it is, the facts on the ground. Torah, though, advises to take one step further back. In other words, Torah is talking about a נזיר, who swears off every and any scintilla of pleasure or hedonism. Therefore Torah says to distance oneself even from grapes. Rashi, however, is only offering sound advice for the common folk, not necessarily a Nazir. In this regard, it makes perfect sense to deprive oneself merely of wine, a euphemism for all alcoholic beverages, but not all grape products as for a Nazir proper.

בהעלתך
ויהי העם כמתאננים

כמתאננים בגימטריא תורה, the antidote, you may say, to complaining and bickering.

On a separate, but equally important, note, the word כמתאננים can be said to be made of two words כמת אננים (corpse; inconsolable mourners). When one complains and bickers he transforms himself into a corpse (figuratively speaking of course) and everyone around, or near and dear to, him into inconsolable mourners, אננים.

שלח לך אנשים ויתרו "את" ארץ כנען

The כלי יקר writes a fascinating thought as follows:

In this פסוק God says to משה, "Send to you men who will scout the land". רשי points out that שלח לך means לדעתך (according to your understanding or at your discretion משה). The כלי יקר adds that in essence what God was saying was, "If it were Me, I would have sent women, not men, because had you done so you wouldn't have had to deal with all the nonsense that followed; women are built differently and are more in love with the Land than their male counterparts."

I happened to have found a רמז לדבריו in the פסוק itself. The "את" in the פסוק is entirely superfluous. In English it's as if it would read, "and they shall scout the the land..." It would have been quite sufficient had the פסוק merely read ויתרו ארץ כנען. However, the "את" could very well serve as a ראי' לדברי כלי יקר as follows: The "את" is in fact extra and unnecessary just as the "men" were extra and unnecessary.

Upon sharing this ווארט with my very dear brother, Dovid, he added the following additional ראי' לדברי כלי יקר from the very same "את", as follows: If we switch the vowels of the word "את" we get "את" as in "OT" or "AHT", meaning "she", the Hebrew feminine "you". And so again, as the כלי יקר points out, God was saying to משה, "and let '**her**' scout the Land of Canaan". (I must humbly defer to my dear brother, because in his interpretation there no longer exists a superfluous "את"; whereas in my interpretation, it still exists but is explained away).

Another thought or proof is the following: The acronym for שלח לך אנשים is שלא (that not). If we, however, modify slightly and insert instead of the word אנשים the word נשים, then for the words שלח לך נשים ויתרו we have the acronym שלנו (ours), the very opposite theme of שלא. So the women fit better than the men.

A follow up to all the above is the following amazing גימטריא: שלח לך + 12 (spies) = נשים (400).

שלח – עלה נעלה וירשנו...כי אכל נוכל לה

עלה נעלה וירשנו is acronym for עניו, and כי is an acronym for כלב and יהושע.

עניוות (humility) is of course what's required to return and report and react as did כלב and יהושע. Humility is what it took to initially conquer the Land, and that same humility (deference to a higher authority; Torah and its dictates) is what is (or will be) required to conquer the Land once again, not pomposity or egocentricity and the like, exactly the type characteristics displayed by her government for better than sixty years, and the reason for our current demise in Our Land.

חקת – נחש נחשת
פכ'א פסוקים ח-ט

ויאמר ה אל משה עשה לך שרף ושים אותו על נס והיה כל הנשוך וראה אותו וחי. ויעש משה נחש נחשת וישמהו על הנס והיה אם נשך הנחש את איש והביט אל נחש נחשת וחי

Besides the obvious question of what need was there for God to have done so in order to achieve healing for His People following the awful plague that decimated tens of thousands – He could have just as well achieved this end in a multitude of other far more practical and simple ways and means (after all He's God), the greater question here is directed toward רשי as follows:

רשי explains that God did not direct Moshe to make a snake of copper, only Moshe used logic in that because God ordered him to make a "snake" (נחש), he figured he would make one of copper (נחשת) because לשון נופל על לשון (in other words, it's an alliteration of sorts). There's only one problem, however. God never told Moshe to make a נחש (snake), but rather שרף (serpent).

Now of course you're going to say that that's only semantics, and you may be correct, and therefore perhaps Moshe was correct in constructing a "snake". The פסוק itself may in fact be sound; the problem here is with רשי. How could have Moshe possibly made such a leap (alliteration) from נחש to נחשת if to begin with נחש was never the command, was never mentioned?!

Many of the commentary address this problem, but not to complete satisfaction. רמב'ן is even more perplexing because of his Rashi version. By the same token, however, this subtle difference in לשון רשי between the conventional version and Ramban is quite telling and is the single greatest catalyst in triggering my theory in addressing the conundrum at issue.

Ramban writes that Rashi writes: "How did Moshe arrive at a copper snake (נחש נחשת)? Because Moshe said, 'God *ordered me* to make a snake, and so I shall make one of copper, because of the alliteration factor – לשון נופל על לשון'." This is not, however, conventional לשון רשי; rather Rashi says: "Moshe said to himself, God *called it* a snake (נחש); I shall then make it of copper (נחשת)." The difference is not mere semantics.

Thus, if we take לשון רשי as accepted, the majority opinion, there's no real issue any longer. Because Rashi doesn't claim that God *ordered* Moshe to make a נחש, for He in fact didn't, and Rashi knows this; after all עשה לך שרף (make for yourself a *serpent*) is what God said to Moshe. God, however, did previously refer to this 'thing', or *called* it, a snake or נחש, as Torah clearly states... וישלח ה' בעם את הנחשים. So Rashi is in fact on the mark.

Nonetheless some may still cast dispersions on my take because after all even though it is true that God references the term נחש He only does so in relation to the plague, not the cure – two distinct נחשים. So how can I say that God calls that healing mechanism a snake, when He ostensibly does not?

The answer is this. The Hebrew word for "called" as described in Rashi is קוראו. This word maintains a double entendre. The regular definition is of courser "called". There is, however, another, quite common, definition: Occurrence, or Event or Happening (e.g. את אשר *יקרא* or והיה כי *תקראינה* מלחמה אתכם באחרית הימים).

Thus, in this context, if we are simply to apply that latter definition, then my theory is further supported and bolstered. After all, the entire snake thing (first the plague and thereafter the cure) was really one big event, one big קוראו. And so God most definitely, at some point during this entire saga, referred to the snake as a *snake* or נחש. (See also ספורנו).

(As an aside, see Caduceus symbol and meaning, later, Item 165.)

בלק – לקב

Rather interesting that when King בלק admonishes Prophet בלעם for blessing the Jews instead of cursing them (for which he had retained him in the first place), he says: לקב איבי לקחתיך (to curse my enemies have I retained you) והנה ברכת ברך (and instead you have blessed them). Notice though that the word לקב (to curse) is the same letters as the word (name) בלק. Furthermore, the perfect symmetrical opposite to the term לקב (to curse) is the term ברך (to bless). Oddly enough ברך shares a numeric value with the words מלך בלק, indicating that where there's a presence of מלך (king), referring of course to the מלך מלכי המלכים הקבה, all בלק and בלעם can do is bless. (On a separate, yet equally amazing, note, בלק בגימטריא מנוול).

הן עם לבדד ישכן (בלק) – לא תתעב אדמי (שופטים)

הן עם לבדד ישכן is translated as "Thus the nation that shall dwell on its own". This is a verse out of the Book of Numbers (23:9), as part of the curses (or blessings) Prophet בלעם heaved upon the Jewish People while in the desert. This verse served as one of the seminal verses for the late great Rabbi Meir Kahane's vehement position that the Jewish People were meant to dwell separately and apart from the rest of the world in their land, the Land of Israel.

Technically, it's not really R' Kahane's חידוש; rather that is in fact the simple definition of these words, certainly if one considers the continuation of that same verse ובגויים לא יתחשב ("and do not mingle, associate or assimilate with the gentiles").

However, R' Meir's approach that supports this position is in fact novel, as follows:

הן (meaning either "thus" or "behold" or "lo"), in this context, is an interesting word. More importantly, however, both these letters ה and נ are unique among Hebrew letters. The numbers 10 and 100 (as well as 1000, 1000,000, though not very germane, as the Hebrew alphabet numerologic rules and practices don't practically play a role in figures above 400 – a topic way beyond the purview of this book) are considered perfect numbers. What is the only number, however, that can be doubled or clone itself in order to achieve these figures? Only "5" or the letter ה (to make "10"), and "50" or letter נ (to make "100"). The idea or analogy then here is that only homogeneous letters ה and נ are in fact עם לבדד ישכן, for they are the only two letters that to reach their desired perfect numbers can only do so by doubling themselves.

I have another fascinating thought that supports the above nicely.

In דברים כג:ח there is another very interesting and somewhat bewildering verse:

לא-תתעב אדמי, כי אחיך הוא (Do not loath the Edomite for he is your brother). What does this verse mean? The Edomite is my brother? Really? Now of course one could answer this question by pointing to the fact that אדום is referring to עשו who was brother to יעקב. It still, however, sounds pretty odd, because so what if the Edomite is my brother? He's a no-goodnik. The צרות we Jews suffered at the hand of the Edomite is indescribable. Even our forefather Jacob suffered miserably from, and lived in fear of, his brother Esau all his life. So what kind of commandment is this?

As it turns out though, אדמי is גימטריא "55", the same as the word הן. Thus what the פסוק is perhaps hinting at is exactly the aforesaid. That is to say, "Do not loathe your own (הן), because he is in fact your brother."

Finally, what is truly amazing is that the word immediately following the title word: הן, is the word עם (nation (of Israel)). The word עם bears the numeric value of 110, exactly double the numeric value of its predecessor: הן. This further hammers home the herein lesson beautifully.

בלק (משיח) דרך כוכב מיעקב

בלק is read alone (without its predecessor, חקת) only when **17** Tammuz (the day marking) falls on שבת; otherwise the two are read together on the same Shabbat. Isn't it then odd that the single verse in all of Torah referencing משיח (the antidote) is to be found in Verse "**17**"?

וגם בלק הלך לדרכו

This language is very interesting and rarely used. The only other place in Torah we find similar text is with regard to Forefather Jacob when he parted from his uncle and father-in-law Lavan. Why does Torah choose to use a similar description with respect to Balak? What even was the need altogether for Torah to relate the fact that Balak went on his way? Seems superfluous.

I believe Torah is hinting at the poetic justice here; the fact that Yaacov actually got the last laugh, the fact that we've come full circle.

My theory is further bolstered by a very interesting repeated reference throughout Bil'am's curse blessings (x4). The Jewish people throughout are always only referred to as Yaacov. It is rather odd that we are referred to in this fashion; it is not very common at all. But in both poetic form (which the curse blessings appear to be) as well as poetic "justice" form, it is perfectly fitting. For it is this constant reference to Jacob and its philology that ties a perfect bow around this Torah portion and its wonderful blessings that were showered upon Bnei Yisroel, the Children of Israel, the children of יעקב.

בעל הטורים על פנחס – זמרי בן סלוא נשיא בית אב

The בעל הטורים writes that שלמיאל is זמרי בן סלוא זה גימטריא. Initially I wasn't sure what was bugging the בעל הטורים, but after some further introspection it appears that he's bothered by the fact that it is previously written in Torah that the chief prince of the tribe of שמעון was שלמיאל בן צורישדי. Here it appears, however, that זמרי is the Tribe's chieftain, and so how do we reconcile this apparent contradiction? Therefore, the בעל הטורים addresses this apparent contradiction by explaining that the names שלמיאל and זמרי בן סלוא + the additional word זה ("this is") possess the same numeric value or גימטריא, perhaps hinting to the fact that the two were the same person.

Considering the source, I was willing to accept this גימטריא on its face. My בר מצוה בחור, however, wasn't. So he calculated the letters' values. Turns out, the גימטריא is in fact off by "7" (quite significant).

I found in various commentary on בעל הטורים that if we add the "ו" to שלמיאל plus we apply the common גימטריא concept of עם הכולל (which says that whenever you are "1" short, it is permissible to simply add the word itself as "1" to reach your desired גימטריא), we've got the missing "7", or 418 on both sides. Alternatively, one may drop the "ו" of סלוא, that only serves as a vowel, and once again with עם הכולל (tweaking "+/-1"), you again have equal numbers, each adding up, in this case, to 412. However, this doesn't satisfy me and shouldn't satisfy anyone else for the following reasons.

First, to begin with עם הכולל is not to be used on a whim or whenever one feels like it; otherwise it becomes cheap and meaningless. I would venture to say that if that is in fact what

בעל הטורים intended he could have and would have clearly said so. He does not.

Second, applying both concepts of מלא and עם הכולל is a stretch. I've never seen this done before and don't believe it is sound.

Third, why then did בעל הטורים spell the name שלמיאל חסר with no "י"? For these reasons, I don't buy the way in which some commentary wish to spin or explain this inexplicable, or certainly awkward, בעל הטורים.

Here, though, are *my* thoughts on resolving this apparent conundrum:

First, we may simply add the ה הידיעה (as in the *notorious* or *infamous*), borrowed from "זה", to זמרי, as in הזמרי, then negate the **"ז"** completely, and problem solved.

If you don't care for my ה הידיעה spin, we may still add the letter "ה" to represent the theme of the ה בית אבות of Tribe שמעון, as Rashi and other commentary explain.

However, although these may seem wonderful sparks of genius in order to fit the גימטריאות, it does nothing to address or answer or explain the בעל הטורים itself. So here are my thoughts on trying to explain this בעל הטורים and what he might have intended.

You know those ads like 1800Mattress (leave off the last "s" for "savings")? Or how about those vanity numbers, like 1800-WIN-A-TRIP? That's eight numbers; there's no such phone number in the world? Seven digits is the standard phone number. So what does it mean when companies have these vanity phone numbers that go eight, nine or even ten digits, just to spell out the name of the company, product or marketing gimmick? It's intended strictly as a mnemonic, but obviously you don't dial all eight numbers, only seven. Besides, on a standard land line, the phone won't allow you to dial any more than seven digits, because once you hit the seventh, it'll patch you into the call, and the phone will begin to ring on the other end. The same is true here.

We remove both the "ו" and "א" from סלוא. This is both reasonable in the greater world, as I have just shown, and it is most certainly fair game and fully permissible in גימטריאות, especially considering another very common idea in Jewish lore and Torah grammar, that of קרי and כתיב (pronounced form versus written form). Though it is written סלוא with "ו" and "א", it may be "read" without either. In other words, even though in Hebrew, there is no concept of vowel letters per se, as we have vowel symbols instead, unlike the English language (A, E, I, O, U, and sometimes Y), there is, nonetheless, even in Hebrew Alphabet, a modicum of vowel letters (א. ה. ו. י. ע). These letters many a time serve no other purpose but as vowels, completely void of a consonant benefit. Therefore, because "ו" and "א" (two vowel letters) in this word (סלוא) strictly serve as vowels, (because one can easily read the name סלוא without the "ו" and "א", and instead just place a קבוץ vowel underneath the "ל", and it would read the very same), we can therefore legitimately remove them without consequence. As a result of removal of these ("ו" and "א"), that add up to "7", all is perfectly well.

Furthermore, generally, if you're going to remove letters, it makes most sense not to remove interior letters, but rather exterior ones, like the "ו" and "א" in this case, certainly when these are not only exterior letters, but the final two of the entire four-word compilation (זה זמרי בן סלוא) that the בעל הטורים references. So the point here then is that in defending the בעהט position it is very reasonable and fitting to assume, as I proffer hereinabove, that his גימטריא was based on the קרי, not כתיב, form of: זה זמרי בן סל-וא.

מטות

The numeric value of גד + ראובן is "בירדן", which is where these two tribes (exclusively) settled or resided (in Jordan).

Also, if we add the two above names, along with the additional "ו" as in גד וראובן, we get the גימטריא of עבר, as in מעבר לירדן (across the Jordan – from Israel proper).

Finally, and probably most fascinatingly, the numeric value of לראובני ולגדי וחצי מנשי (for half Tribe מנשה also resided in Jordan alongside their two cousins) is "מעבר לירדן מזרחה".

פנחס-מטות – בנות צלפחד
בנות בגימטריא "נחת"

שופטים – בנה בית...נטע כרם...ארש אשה

רמבם הל' דעות פ'ה ה'יא writes, that the proper or most ideal order of business for a mature adult is to first solidify a livelihood, then to construct a home, and only thereafter to marry. As proof he cites the פסוקים referencing same in שופטים פ'. He says that in שופטים we've got ומי האיש אשר נטע כרם, מי האיש אשר בנה בית, ומי האיש אשר ארש אשה (He who plants a vineyard – a euphemism for livelihood; He who builds a home; He who marries). There's only one problem with this רמבם – that is not the פסוקים order of שופטים (the order rather is בית, כרם, אשה). How do we reconcile this?

The כסף משנה, the פרי חדש and others offer interesting perspectives, but do not directly address the real dilemma. They seem to address the רמבם order, period. (In other words, why he chose the order he did). They do not, however, address the far more pressing question of how it is that רמבם "proof" for his order is completely askew and incorrect.

I posed this question to many a person and mostly received blank stares. I decided to pose the question to my Bar Mitzvah son's, Mendel's, class. Two boychiks came up with interesting answers, but once again, like the כסף משנה and others, only addressed the secondary question of the order, but not the "proof" for the order. They, nonetheless, have earned honorable mention herein, as follows:

הר' הב' ר' יהושע סערעברבריאנסקי said that because שופטים is referring to wartime, רמבם wishes to convey how things ought to be during normal peace time, thus he reverses it.

My nephew הר' הב' ר' לייב פולטר said, רמבם is being very practical. One first requires money, and thus a livelihood, in order to build a home. Therefore he precedes "home-building" with "livelihood".

But then ר' לייב, with help of an elder scholar, his Rebbe (teacher), Rabbi E. Jacobowitz, בשם שערי אהרן בשם חתם סופר בשם מהרי אדרב'י, opined the following truly original fresh approach, as follows:

שופטים contemplates נטע רבעי[7], therefore the פסוק mentions the term ולא חללו which would only apply to נטע רבעי. Hence,

---

[7] A Torahdic מצוה beyond the purview of this Book.

during the first three years when enjoying the fruits (or wine) of the vineyard is *Halachically* prohibited, he's instead busy building his home; only thereafter is he permitted to partake of the vineyard (in year four). So in truth, says רמבם (though it is not apparent to the untrained eye), there is a silent פסוק, if you will, between פסוקים ד and ה. Torah, however, need not clearly spell out this silent verse because it is obvious, especially when it later uses the term ולא חללו, that in fact a *planting* of the vineyard had to have taken place beforehand, four years beforehand. Therefore רמבם proof is actually spot on. Even according to Torah the order of business is in fact as רמבם posits. It's just that Torah is more preoccupied and interested in teaching us a double lesson, that of נטע רבעי as well. It, therefore, squeezes in ו פסוק between ה' and ז'. But in the ideal world, it is self understood that there was already a "planting" of the vineyard beforehand, before the בנה בית (building of the home), just as רמבם writes.

I've come up with the following out-of-the-box novel approach in answering this conundrum.

What is the entire thrust of הל' דעות to begin with? What is the primary concern or focus of the רמבם in this section of his monumental work יד החזקה? Not to deviate far left or far right but that the optimal path to take is the דרך אמצעי or דרך בינוני, the middle ground. This is a theme that cuts through the entire הל דעות.

Furthermore, this specific הלכה is apparently the mother of all הל' דעות for it is the only הלכה that begins with the words דרך בעלי דעה, indicating that this is *the* הלכה of *the* epitome of בעלי דעה. Thus it stands to reason that רמבם chooses his order accordingly, because within the three-פסוקים series, כרם or livelihood is the center one, the entire purpose and theme of הל דעות and בעלי דעה.

Therefore, it stands to reason that not only did Rambam choose his order wisely, but that his order is in fact perfectly aligned with Torah. How so? Because Rambam himself didn't get his idea of דרך אמצעי out of a hat; he didn't concoct it out of thin air. Rather it has a basis in Torah itself, and here we have clear proof therefor. So Rambam's proof from Torah is in fact spot on. Because if we follow Rambam's logic in that *middle* is optimal, then *Karem* ought be first.

It should be further noted that as fate would have it, הל׳ דעות itself is sandwiched between two תורה: They are הל׳ יסודי התורה and הל׳ תלמוד תורה, further bolstering my theory hereinabove. In other words, רמבם purposely fit דעות between both הל׳ תורה (one "foundations" thereof, the other "study" thereof) to in fact teach us, even subliminally, that this should be the aspiration of, and ideal emulation for, a true Torah Jew – the middle path.

(On an aside, although it does seem so, I don't believe רמבם had intended for his citing the פסוקים to serve as proof of his order as much as of the central idea of these three items. I say so only because רמבם, when citing, clearly states the פסוקים perfectly accurately, even grammatically; i.e. ומי האיש (**and** if a man). Certainly, the רמבם knew that when a פסוק begins with ו׳ החיבור this means that something came before it. And yet he ignores whatever came before it. If anything, I'd venture to say that the only proof his Torah order serves is with regard to אשה, the last item of business, which position order everyone agrees on – last).

(One final point: רמבם, after delineating his order, uses the term שנאמר (as it is written), a common term indicating "proof therefor". However, this is not really the term used; it is rather our interpretation of the term he uses. In the original version of רמבם, this term is abbreviated as in שנ׳. Perhaps רמבם intended this as an abbreviation for the word שנה (to change or modify, i.e. the order of) and not שנאמר, the term we commonly apply to this abbreviation, and as perhaps in this case was applied in error. (I know it's a stretch, but there are certainly grounds upon which to make this argument). (Also see כמוצא שלל רב on this topic).

שופטים
עגלה ערופה – וענו ואמרו

רש׳י asks: Would one even suspect the Elders of murder, so that the verse need dictate a short recitation for the elders during the עגלה ערופה ritual that in essence vindicates them? Oddly enough, however, the terminology רש׳י uses to ask the question is וכי עלתה על לב... (*Would it arise upon your heart?*) This is awkward terminology or expression. If at all, רש׳י should have written וכי עלתה על ראש or וכי עלתה על מח (*Would it even enter your* **head** *or* **mind?**) What's the *heart* all about? Nobody's *heart* suspects; one's *head* doubts or questions or ponders. So then why does רש׳י specifically choose to use the term על לב?

I think I may have found an answer:

As it turns out, the first word of the subject פסוק is וענו which possesses a numeric value of "על לב". What is the significance of this גימטריא? It teaches a threefold lesson, as follows:

1. To show that only this פסוק is singled out and no other. In other words, the other eight פסוקים which explain the entire process and procedure of the עגלה ערופה continue unabated even if Torah did not impose the elders' recitation of the פסוק וענו. That is to say that regardless of one's personal feelings about this procedure or the Elders requirement to recite such awkward verbiage, the מצוה of עגלה ערופה still continues and would not be preempted under any circumstance. (In legalese, this would be similar to a contract where there's a catch-all boilerplate provision in which it is clearly stated that if and when one clause or provision of the contract shall be rendered inapplicable, unenforceable and or illegal, this should not

impact the entire contract, and that all other provisions and terms shall remain in full force and effect).

2. וענו also spells the word ענוו (humble). It takes humility of the "heart" to first appreciate the need to comply and recite the verse, and secondly, it takes the same humility of the "heart" to avoid or prevent such matters, such senseless murder, from repeating.

3. If you take this murder "to heart" (על לב) then you'll be assured that in fact these incidents will not repeat.

בן סורר ומורה – פ׳ תצא

The בעה׳ט writes that "סורר" בגימטריא "זה אבשלום בן דויד"

בעל הטורים is off by "1", which is of course common and permissible in גימטריאות (as related multiple times above – עם הכולל).

I, however, have come up with a perfect solution. Remove זה and the extra "י" of דויד, and replace with one fitting word: "אך", as in אך אבשלום בן דוד (only Absalom son of David), and you've got a perfect גימטריא match with סורר, without the need for the use of עם הכולל. The "אך" of course telling us that אבשלום is the "only" truly defined בן סורר ומורה in the Torah.

פ' תצא
יבם

יבם בגימטריא בן, which is the entire purpose of the מצוה in the first place.

פ' תבוא
ושמת בטנא

The word "בטנא" posseses a numeric value of "62", the very number of פסוקים between ששי and שביעי, minus the final פסוק סט that is anyhow not part of the curses, but is rather a catchall פסוק at the very end of the תוכחה.

This of course hints to the fact that the טנא מלא ברכות (basket laden with blessings), that the פרשה opens with, will overwhelm and will envelope the קללות or תוכחה too (62 vs. 62). Even in the תוכחה God will not forsake us, because He loves us too much.

כי תבוא (תוכחה)
"כי תבוא" בגימטריא "תוכחה"

נצבים – ר'ה

Considering that this פרשה is always read the Shabbos immediately preceding ראש השנה, it is fitting then that the word נצבים has a numeric value of קצב or 192.

First, קצב means "apportion" or "allocate" which we know is one of the chief things Hashem is busy with on ראש השנה; that is to apportion or affix one's livelihood or financial wherewithal for the coming year. Further highlighting this point is the fact that if we switch the letter order of this word, we get בצק (dough), which in slang or common parlance/vernacular is defined as "money" (or livelihood – פרנסה). Finally, if we switch the letter order once again, we get קבץ, which means "to gather", which is really what happens on ר'ה ויו'כ as we gather all together in שול, and as God gathers us all in, and embraces us with love and tenderness, as we return *home*, and once again beseech our King to continue to reign over us for another year.

נצבים – וחיית ורבית

רש״י on these words writes הרי חיים (this is life). It is therefore interesting to note that the first of the above title's two-word set (וחיית) is the same numeric value (434) as the word "תלד" (to give birth or life, as specifically referenced in שמות regarding the great midwives שפרה ופועה). The second word "ורבית" (618) has the same numeric value as the words כי הם חיינו וארך ימינו ובהם נהגה (for these are your life and the length of your days and in them ye shall immerse yourself) – referring to the study of Torah and the performance of her mitzvoth. In other words, one hints to "physical" life, while the other to "figurative" or "spiritual" life.

וילך
לֹא אוּכַל עוֹד לָצֵאת וְלָבוֹא וַיהֹוָה אָמַר אֵלַי לֹא תַעֲבֹר אֶת הַיַּרְדֵּן הַזֶּה (דברים לא:ב)

What exactly did Moshe mean with this admonition? לא אוכל עוד לצאת ולבא (I cannot go or come)?

There is really here a double entendre, as follows: משה didn't merely mean "I can't go or come", for what was the point in him relating this to the Jewish people? Of what benefit were these words? Of course certain commentary write that משה was not referring to a physical handicap, but rather to a spiritual or figurative handicap. In other words, משה was saying, "the baton has now been passed on (to my successor יהושע); therefore I am spiritually unable to further serve you or shepherd you as I have for forty years – there's a new sheriff in town"

Though this is a wonderful explanation, I've come up with what, I'd like to believe, is a novel approach, as follows:

The פסוק ought to have said לא יכול, as in modern-day Hebrew vernacular. What's לא אוכל?

What משה was in essence saying was something completely different.

You recall back in the Book of שמות in the portion of שמות where it all began? Where did it really all begin? Very good: The Burning Bush. And what does תורה write there? והסנה איננו אכל (the Bush did not burn up, did not disintegrate, as it naturally should have). Do you see the same word in both instances? אכל and אוכל? Moses was connecting the beginning to the end, from where it all began forty years earlier till today when he's about to pass on to greener pastures – full circle. Thus really these are not words of sorrow or grief; rather they are words of encouragement. "We've come full circle, boys, and just as והסנה איננו אכל way back when we first met, so too now nothing's changed, לא אוכל, that Bush that represents everything good and everything Godly has to date not been consumed and won't ever." The fact that the following word in the *pasuk*, עוד, bears the numeric value of "80", the very age Moshe was when he first encountered the Burning Bush and began his loyal leadership of his people, only further supports my premise. Moreover, the word הסנה possesses a numeric value (גימטריא) of "120", the years of Moshe's life, the age he is right at this moment as he is about to depart from earth.

וַיהוָה אָמַר אֵלַי לֹא תַעֲבֹר אֶת הַיַּרְדֵּן הַזֶּה "and furthermore," continues Moshe, "and it was already pre-destined back then, God had already told me back then לֹא תַעֲבֹר אֶת הַיַּרְדֵּן הַזֶּה, I will not cross the Jordan into the Promised Land. So don't be dejected now that it's time for me to move on to another dimension and that I may not join or lead you into the Land, for that privilege, that merit, was destined for my successor, Joshua."

One last point is that some may ask, but why the additional letter ו in our אוכל? I'm not sure this requires an answer, but I'll certainly take a stab at it.

The letter "ו", as related in קבלה, represents the idea of המשכה מלמעלה למטה, extension or conduit from above to below through which God feeds and sustains us with His glory (already mentioned earlier in several other anecodtes). We are well aware that משה was the first to achieve this great feat, to draw down God's grace into this world. Therefore it stands to reason that though it may have begun (at the סנה espisode) אכל void of ו, after forty years of loyal service Moshe certainly achieved the awesome המשכה, as hinted in the revised spelling of אוכל here (at the end of his life).

האזינו – יערף

The word יערף is a wonderful רמז to the authenticity of תושבע'פ, and that it is indeed divinely inspired, if not divinely gifted, just like תושב'כ.

Rashi, and other commentary, writes that the term יערף refers to something that descends. רש'י, and other commentary, says further that the following word לקחי refers to תורה; in other words Torah that descended from on high to this mundane world.

My added spin regarding תושבע'פ is that the word יערף = 360 or ש'ס (ששה סדרים – תושבע'פ).

SECTION I – (b)

שבת

שבת is the greatest gift God has given the Jewish people. It is the essence of love between God and His people, as we recite throughout our שבת prayers, liturgy and hymns. It is the love between the groom (God) and His bride (Israel); the idea of שבת כלה or שבת מלכה. Thus, it is quite fascinating, among many other acronyms for the word שבת, that one in particular truly depicts this concept, this idea of amorous and of deep-seeded love of God toward the Jewish people as represented in the שבת.

In פרקי אבות (Ethics of our Fathers), the משנה tells us that there are two types of "love", and that one type is far greater than the other. One is אהבה שהיא תלויה בדבר (a love contingent on something). The other is אהבה שאינה תלויה בדבר (a love not contingent on anything). The latter is of course the greater of the two, and perhaps the greatest form of all love.

שבת is an acronym for שאינה תלויה בדבר – the latter one above, the greater one, perhaps the greatest.

NOTE OF PREEMPTION: A smart Alec may turn the question back to me as follows: "Wait a minute, isn't שהיא תלויה בדבר also an acronym for שבת?" Good point. However, though it is true that both אהבות are indeed ר"ת שבת; nonetheless, three things: First, because the former אהבה, the שהיא תלויה בדבר, may be transformed into a contraction, as in שתלויה בדבר, whereas the latter, שאינה תלויה בדבר, may not be, it is more sensible to apply the ר"ת to the latter, שאינה תלויה בדבר. Second, the word שאינה contains the letters that make up the entire word for ש, (as in ש י נ), the first letter of the word שבת; not so with the word שהיא. Third, and finally, the word שאינה also contains the letters that make up the word שינה (sleep), which is a big part of the שבת

(as in the acronym: שינה בשבת תענוג). After all, שבת means rest (relaxation).

שבת...מבני היקר הב"ם מנחם מענדל

שבת בגימטריא תקרב (to come close or nearby), because שבת is the quintessential closeness or bonding between God and His Chosen People.

תשרי

תשרי is an acronym for its first two ימים טובים, which are of course יו"כ and ר"ה. How?

תשרי ר"ת תקיעה שברים תרועה (ר"ה) י (יו"כ)

ערב ראש השנה

As fate would have it, the ר"ת of ערב ראש השנה is ערה (awaken), which is the entire purpose and thrust of the entire month of

אלול culminating or climaxing on ערב ראש השנה, the final day of אלול.

Now of course those letters may also spell other (negative) words, like רעה (bad), or הרע (the bad), but only if you twist the letters out of order. And that is exactly the lesson of אלול and ערב ראש השנה and ראש השנה itself. You stay on the straight and narrow, you'll be fine – you'll truly be awakened and invigorated. If, however, you deviate, from even something as seemingly harmless as an acronym that spells out the eve of the first of the Jewish new-year, you may be writing yourself a life sentence, (perhaps a death sentence).

ערוב תבשילין

The first four words of this short liturgical rite recited on the eve of certain holidays for purposes of allowing cooking and general food preparation on יום טוב are בדין יהא שרא לנא, acronym בישל (cooking).

Upon sharing this ווארט with a dear and clever חבר, however, he pointed out an "interesting" flaw, as follows: עירובי חצרות and עירובי תחומין (neither having anything to do with cooking or permissibility of food preparation on יום טוב) as well begin with the very same words. I'm still not sure though that it totally discounts my ווארט. However, it certainly deserves further introspection.

I therefore propose a challenge to my reading audience. Whoever turns in the best answer to this apparent conundrum, shall receive $180, plus five (5) free autographed TAVLINs, as well as honorable mention in the reprint version of this book. Please email your answers to: editor@davidharppublishers.com

יום כפור
אם יהיו חטאיכם כשנים...[8]

אם יהיו חטאיכם כשנים כשלג ילבינו אם יאדימו כתולע כצמר יהיו (If your sins shall be like red thread, I shall whiten them like snow; if they shall redden like a worm, as [white as] wool shall they become).

This פסוק has long perplexed me.

What's the significance of the double expression and why the variation in prose from the רישא to the סיפא?

What it appears to me is as follows: The whitening in the רישא is far more severe and therefore far more impactful than the whitening in the סיפא. For in the רישא the terminology used is ילבינו, the equivalent of when one koshers utensils through the process of לבון (purifying an item by directed fire for an extended period of time till the item turns "red" hot). Whereas the סיפא speaks of no formal whitening process; rather simply "white as wool *shall they become*" or יהיו. If this is in fact the case, then it's important, I think, to further study this פסוק in greater depth to better gain a firm understanding of the significance of the two different terms, for we assume, that these terms or prose are not merely so placed for purposes of poetry or to dazzle the reader.

It would further appear that the sins discussed in the רישא are milder than those discussed in the סיפא, because as we said earlier, the term יהיו is passive – simply defined as "become" of its own accord. In the סיפא, however, we find a far harsher sin term: יאדימו כתולע (when they 'redden' like a worm).

---

[8] ראה גם רמבם טומאת אוכלין פרק ב הלכה כג: רמבם תשובה פרקים ה-ו: מסכת יומא פרק ו: חפץ חיים על התורה פרשת וארא ד"ה ואני אקשה לב פרעה: מיכה חמש פסוקים האחרונים עם המלבים על אתר

Thus now things begin to fall into place.

In fact, what God is saying to us is that *if in fact your sins are merely minor indiscretions, I shall whiten them as snow, for snow is from above, from God. And so I shall, with proper and sincere* תשובה *of course, correct these. In the case, however, where the human really strayed afar and "reddened" those sins to a severe degree, then* כצמר יהיו *(like wool they shall become)*. Wool is from a sheep, it is grounded; it is down here on earth with us (unlike snow). Sheep is also the prototype for קרבנות (animal sacrifices), the one true path back to God following a transgression.

So in קבלה terms, we'd call the רישא אתערותא דלעילא (a heavenly or supernal or Godly awakening or inspiration); whereas the סיפא we'd refer to as אתערותא דלתתא (an earthly or human awakening or inspiration).

Therefore, we will also find that in the case of the רישא, God promises whitening *through snow*. Snow covers up, snow masks or camouflages; whereas the סיפא term indicates more one of merely "I will make as if (it's not there), but of course it still will be." Because, after all, man, try as he may, does not carry the weight or power God does, and so his power to repent or his power to achieve complete and everlasting erasure of sin is not equivalent to God's. At the same time, however, God is only able to cure the mildly sick, the רישא sins we discussed earlier, the more mild ones; the big peccadillos, those contemplated in the סיפא, can only be rectified by man alone; man alone must make amends.

A final note: The word צמר (the above latter term) is only 3 short (numerically) from the word שלג (the above former term). This, I think, hints to the three paths of true penance: תשובה תפילה צדקה. This then tells us that, accompanied with these three forms of repentance, God is certain to cleanse us with "snow", with "true" and everlasting absolution and forgiveness, further hinted in the גימטריא of שלג. Because...

$$\text{במספר קטן "שלג" בגימטריא "אמת"}$$
$$\text{שלג} = 3+3+3 = 9$$
$$\text{אמת} = 4+4+1 = 9$$

Yizkor (יזכור)

I have decoded the word יזכור to spell out the four times per year we recite the prayer (a mnemonic if you will), as follows:

The י in the word יזכור represents either the **10**th of the Hebrew month of תשרי or the first letter of the holiday on which we first recite this prayer, יום כפור.

The ו represents the **6**th of the Hebrew month of סיון on which we celebrate the holiday of שבועות, and on which of course we once again intone the יזכור prayer.

The כר combine to give us a numeric value of **220**. If we apply the concept of מספר קטן we get **22** (because we drop the "0"), which represents the 22nd of the Hebrew month of ניסן, or אחרון של פסח, on which once again we recite the יזכור service[9].

Finally, the ז either stands for the seventh Hebrew month, תשרי, in which we find the final holiday, שמע׳צ, on which we recite יזכור. Or, if we wish to stretch it a bit further, Hebrew letter ז is pronounced *zayin*. You cannot spell letter ז without the Hebrew letter ע (*ayin*); letter ע of course representing the initial of that final holiday, עצרת.

---

[9] This does beg the question, how about in Israel where only one day of Passover is observed and so the recitation of יזכור occurs a day earlier, on the 21st? As of yet, I have not arrived at a solution to this problem.

יזכור

This ווארט may be unique to נוסח אריז"ל, though I wouldn't be surprised if it were applicable to other נוסחאות as well (specifically, variations of נוסח ספרד), but I haven't found any yet. Still, though the ווארט has merit most particularly with respect to נוסח ארי, nonetheless it is my firm opinion that everyone will enjoy it.

We find something very unique about חב"ד or its נוסח יזכור, as follows:

We know that generally, aside from עלי' לתורה, whenever one is mentioned for a holy ritual rite or for a מי שברך it is שמו ושם אמו (individual's name son/daughter of mom) as in פלוני בן פלונית. However, posthumous references are always שמו ושם אביו (individual's name son/daughter of dad), except in נוסח ארי יזכור. Why? Of course that's a rhetorical question as no one has thus far been able to offer any answer, let alone any sound answer. So I thought hard and long about this and here's what I came up with.

Two reasons:

1. What is the יזכור prayer anyhow? What's the entire thrust, the entire point and purpose of this תפלה? It's all about the fact that we ask Hashem to remember our loved ones (parents) עם נשמות אברהם יצחק יעקב שרה רבקה רחל ולאה, (along with the souls of our forefathers and foremothers), i.e. our Jewish heritage, the fact that we are the children of Abraham, Isaac, Jacob, et al. And who determines this? Who determines that we are in fact the children of these great personalities, of these

monumental figureheads? Who determines we are Jewish? Mom. Thus it stands to reason that we carve out a special exception for this prayer only, and that even posthumously reference mom, not dad.

2. [A bit more contorted, but far more impressive]. What is the only holiday on which we don't recite יזכור? Correct, ראש השנה. Why not? Ever dawned on you to ask 'why not'? Good question, isn't it? Well my theory is because ראש השנה is *the* יזכור of the year. How so? Because after all, doesn't its name say it all? What's the truly Torahdic name for this holiday? Correct again, יום הזכרון; in other words, the mother (no pun intended) of all Yizkors, all זכרונות. Therefore, it supersedes the need for all other recitations thereof, because on its own the entire holiday is the consummate יזכור.

Now let me ask you this: On ראש השנה exactly what are we *yizkoring*? Yes, I know about the verse זה היום תחלת מעשיך זכרון ליום ראשון, but first what does that verse even mean? Second, there is a far greater memorial theme on this holiday, one that is euphemistically scribbled all over the pages of the מחזור.

Whom does God remember in the תורה readings of ראש השנה? Whom does He remember in the *haftorot*? שרה הגר רחל חנה ואמא דסיסרא (Sarah, Hagar, Rachel, Hanna, Mother of General Cisero). And what do these women have in common? Correct again, they're all "mothers", and they are *remembered* in their capacity as "mothers". Thus, it stands to reason that if in fact ראש השנה, the mother of all Yizkors, as we have just established, is all about *yizkoring* mom, then the very brief 2-minute prayer (of same name and theme) we recite on all the other holidays ought to follow suit and theme – MOM. Thus the שמו ושם אמו mention even posthumously (in יזכור).

סוכות - אתרוג
פרי עץ הדר

Isn't it odd that nowhere in the Torah is there any reference to or mention of אתרוג? Rather, all Torah says is that we should acquire (during the סוכות holiday) a פרי עץ הדר.

I have a theory about this.

פרי עץ הדר (659) has a numeric value exactly 49 greater than אתרוג (610). What this then tells us is that only if and when we have in fact taken an אתרוג for "seven" days (the Torahdic requirement) and we have further flawlessly executed all the great מחשבות ועבודה related to, and encompassed within, it, and have thus permeated all the seven מדות of (חגת נהים), and as "seven" is כלול in "seven" (just as in ספירת העומר) = 49, only then have we indeed achieved and affected the title or level of פרי עץ הדר (a truly magnificent and aesthetically pleasing fruit; i.e. that to which "God" is magnificent and pleasing). Until then though אתרוג is just that – an אתרוג, nothing more.

הלל

הלל בגימטריא *סה* or "65". If we reverse סה, we get הס as in הס קטיגור (hush prosecutor), part of our ראש השנה and יו'כ liturgy. This is the great crowning achievement of שבח והלל להקב'ה

(singing God's praises); that He silences the evil angels, the bad guys.

Further bolstering this point: The end of that line of acrostic poetry is וקח סניגור (and welcome the defense attorney), which is a continuation of course of what we plead with God to do during the Ten Days of Awe.

וקח בגימטריא קיד, the very chapter of תהילים in which you will find the הלל.

הושענא רבה

"הושענא רבה" בגימטריא "גמרת" (finish or conclude), which is a wonderful clue to what this day is all about and what it represents. Because as we know הושענא רבה is the true and final completion or culmination of the entire אלול, רה ויוכ.

A further interesting thought that hammers home this point is that whereas the word גמר is to finish or to complete and is a word commonly used in אלול רה ויוכ vernacular, as when we wish each other גמר טוב (a good ending) or גמר חתימה טובה (a good completed seal), the "ת" is actually the final letter of the א-ב, ultimately *completing* the entire Aleph-Bet, a greater sense of completion, a more complete finality.

פורים – המלך:המן

Just interesting to note that המלך and המן share the numeric value of 95. Not sure what to make of this, but there must be something very telling.

פסח – והיא שעמדה

והיא (and she) refers to the Torah who has withstood the test of time. Interestingly, it contains the גימטריא 22, representing the 22 Hebrew alphabets (כב אותיות התורה).

Furthermore, the גימטריא of והיא שעמדה is 441, the גימטריא of the word אמת (truth). Torah is "true". The fact that we have withstood this long is "true". The fact that Torah is the primary, if not exclusive, reason that we have withstood this long, in spite of the והיא שעמדה paragraph's contents is once again אמת.

שבועות
כפה עליהם הר כגיגית (טעם לחלבי)

There are many reasons we eat dairy on שבועות. Most of us only know about 4-5 reasons, but would you believe it if I told you there are in fact tens?

But let's at least focus on the most popular or common ones:
1. Included in the Torah, that the Jews received at Mt. Sinai on this lovely holiday, is the Mitzvah of Kashrut (kosher dietary laws). Part of kosher dietary laws is the law pertaining to proper preparation of livestock and meat products for consumption. As the Jews heretofore did not follow these laws (because they had not yet received the Torah) their meat and all cookware and utensils were rendered unkosher. Thus, the only alternative was to eat dairy instead, which does not require any advance preparation or complex laws.

    (As an addendum to this first reason, however, a question follows: Why didn't the Jews then simply slaughter new livestock and kosher the pots and utensils according to the dictates of Torah? The answer is that the revelation at Sinai (that year שבועות) fell on Shabbat, a day on which, unlike the holidays (when falling on regular weekdays), cooking or koshering or even slaughtering is strictly prohibited).

2. Torah is akin to milk, as it is written, "Like honey and milk [the Torah] lies under your tongue."

3. The numeric value of the word "milk" in Hebrew (חלב) is "40", representing: (1) 40 days Moses spent on the Mountain to receive the Torah. (2) The number

of years the Jews spent in the desert. (3) The number of generations from Moses (recorder of the Written Law) to רבינא and ר' אשי (recorders and codifiers of the Oral Law or Talmud). (4) "40" is represented by the Hebrew letter *mem*, the letter that both opens and closes the Talmud – the Talmud really incorporating the entire corpus of all of Torah over a period of 1800 years.

4. Another name for Mt. Sinai is הר גבנונים, the mountain of majestic peaks. So this one's somewhat of an alliteration of sorts. The Hebrew word for cheese is גבינה – etymologically, at least, related to Mt. Sinai in its גבנונים reference.

5. On שבועות (in the Temple) the Jews brought a sacrifice to God known as the מנחה חדשה לה' בשבועותיכם. The acronym of the words חדשה לה' בשבועותיכם is Hebrew letters ח, ל, ב (milk).

There are of course others, but the above is a fairly good list of the most acceptable ones, and those that most of us are familiar with.

I have, however, come up with a 6th (and truly wonderful) one, as follows:

First, by way of introduction, it is said that following the Jews' unified pronouncement of נעשה ונשמע (we will do and we will listen), God still found it necessary to כפה עליהם הר כגיגית (lift the Mountain and hoist it up high atop the entire Nation and threaten it: "Either you accept unconditionally or you're doomed right here right now; I shall make this your grave!") Of course the question is why the need for God to have done so, after the Jews ostensibly had already willingly accepted? And the answer is that with that threat God was really bonding Himself to His people. In other words, today they may have accepted the yoke of Torah, but tomorrow may be different. Therefore, God forces it upon them, so that even when and if the Jewish People should ever get the urge to slough off or to simply voluntarily walk away, they cannot because now after the threat, a bond was formed so "go as you may you shall never go astray", perhaps more so for God's sake than for ours. He cannot nor will not ever abandon us regardless of our less than stellar behavior at times.

I thought about this premise hard and long, and found that as fate would have it, the numeric value of the words הר כגיגית is equivalent to the numeric value of the word "תמורה" which means "in exchange for" or "in trade of". Because what relieved God and what convinced Him to spare the Jews and replace the Mountain back on its range, instead of burying the Jews within its confines, was the Jewish people guaranteeing their children "in exchange" for the Torah. So the "תמורה" of the הר כגיגית threat was the children, the ones עם ישראל pledged to maintain and preserve God's Torah until the end of days, and the only deal or exchange that impressed God enough, ultimately achieving His return of composure and the Mountain.

But there's more.

The numeric value of הר כגיגית is also equivalent to that of the word תרומה (obviously the same letters as the word תמורה above, only slightly different letter order). תרומה means to raise and lift up, which is in essence what God had physically done with the Mountain. But let's not only use this word negatively or physically; let's rather use it as well positively or figuratively, because the connotation is clearly present. That is to say, that through Hashem lifting (תרומה) the Mountain above the heads of the Jewish People, He ultimately brought out the best in them (or us); "lifted" them, "raised" them above the fray in two ways. First, above the fray of the other nations of the world because at the very moment that we committed we became the עם בוחר (Chosen Nation); and second, above the fray in comparison to what we would have been with only the נעשה ונשמע, minus the כפה עליהם, minus sacrificing our children, the perpetual guarantors of the Torah and its Mitzvot – He made us *better*. He made us *purer*. He *made* us.

Now returning to that with which I began: A sixth reason for dairy on שבועות.

הר כגיגית bears the numeric value as well of *Torah* + the letter מ (651). מ is of course "40", the numeric value of the word חלב (as above). (See also תניא, Ch. 47).

Finally, an item that rounds out all the above beautifully:

On page 42 of Tractate סוטה (which, once again as fate would have it, many have the custom of reviewing and studying between Pesach and שבועות), the Talmud writes that Goliath maintained his standoff with King Saul's army for forty (40) days. רש"י explains that the reason Goliath was able to taunt and menace the Jews for forty (40) days is due to the forty-day tarry of the Torah atop Mt. Sinai. Thus Goliath had the requisite powers (from קליפה of course) to at least draw into battle or stalemate the Jews and exhaust them for forty (40) days – in other words, the letter *mem* in our anecdotal exegesis hereinabove. Yet, what is even further astonishing and more than mere fate is that Torah ultimately triumphs over Goliath and over "40", over the letter *mem*. And who was the one to ultimately cause the grand and unlikely victory over the monolithic Goliath? None other than star of the holiday we celebrate today, the בעל ההילולא, the great, indomitable King David, grandchild of that truly divine delightful woman, Ruth, whom we of course as well celebrate and whose book as well we read today. (See also שבת: פח).

שבועות

כתר = רות + דוד. We may say that either רות completed דוד and enabled the כתר that ultimately crowned דוד as king of Israel. We may as well say that the two combined to achieve the ultimate כתר,

the כתר תורה, on this wonderful holiday, the holiday on which all these personalities and concepts are most pronounced. Finally, we may also say that the two combine to make 620 (כתר), equivalent to מצוות דאוריתא ורבנן.

שבועות – אין טוב אלא תורה

אין (pronounced ayin) means "nothing" or "nothingness" or "void". טוב אלא bears the numeric value of 49. Now if we put it all together, we get a very organized order of operation or implementation, as follows:

First there was nothing (אין), then came "49" days (the counting of the עומר the Jews employed from the date of their exodus (פסח) until שבועות, 49 days later), after which time they were gifted with the תורה. So...

1. אין (nothing; pre Torah)
2. טוב אלא (which is "49")
3. תורה (Torah)

Along these lines, there is a baffling בעה'ט in בראשית א:ב.

He writes that the words והארץ היתה תהו ובהו (and the world was barren or desolate; frighteningly empty) is גימטריא of אלפים שנה בלי תורה (two-thousand years without Torah). Like so many בעה'ט, this equation doesn't quite jibe mathematically. The former term = 1152; while the latter term = 1169, a difference of "17".

The only way I can see in which to reconcile the apparent discrepancy is with my brief exegesis above, as follows: טוב is "17". And we know אין טוב אלא תורה. So in fact what בעה'ט is saying is that indeed the two terms share גימטריאות. How so? Because in this specific case, he wished to as well send a very subtle clue to the fact that והארץ היתה תהו ובהו (the earth was astonishingly empty) was only due to its lack of תורה (for 2000 years) אלפים שנה בלי תורה, and because אין טוב אלא תורה it was of course lacking טוב (goodness), or "17", as well. Therefore, the discrepancy is clearly intentional, and is mathematically sound.

שבועות – אין שמחה אלא תורה

I came up with an interesting ראיה to this statement or מאמר חזל.

שמחה בגימט׳ גשן. Goshen of course was the city wherein the eleven brothers and father Jacob settled after they descended to Egypt due to the famine in Canaan. There, Rashi and other commentary write, Jacob and his sons founded ישיבות and בתי מדרש from which Torah (esoterically speaking of course, because this occurred pre-Torah) would thereafter flow forth.

חזון – תשעה באב

The word חזון bears the numeric value of 70[10]. This is of course a רמז to the 70 years the Jews would spend in גלות בבל, their first formal גלות.

---

[10] Though not exactly 70 (rather 71) it is commonly acceptable in גימטריאות to deviate by one. Besides, we may argue it is actually perfectly equal, as the Jews first began returning to their homeland, Israel, in the 71st year.

Also, as this is the הפטרה of שבת חזון, the Shabbat that precedes the most tragic day in the Jewish calendar, תשעה באב, it is further fitting that prophet Isaiah, who prophesieses herein of the destruction of Jeruaslem and her Temple, bears a name that is a further clue to the morass of exile in general. ישעיה could be said to be a combination of two words: יש יה (there is a God). However, notice that there's one more letter (ע) right in the center of the name, separating these two words. In other words, Isaiah was as well hinting to the fact that though while in exile it may appear He's not with us (there is, God-forfend, no God), know that He is; it is just that due to difficult times and sheer exhaustion of what we've endured over the years, we, His children, may from time-to-time get the impression that He is not; the ע (representing the idea of גלות, as it was the number of years of our first) blurring or conealing the otherwise glaring message that יש י-ה (God is indeed alive and well, here with us in these dark times). The greatest proof of this is that the פסוק referencing the fact that God is always with us, even in the kremotoria of Auschwitz, is עמי אנכי בצרה (I am with you in your time of distress). That term or expression or פסוק begins of course with that ever illusive letter ע, perhaps countering the above obstructing one.

SECTION I – (c)

פרקי אבות
Ethics of the Fathers

פ'א מ'א
משה קבל...ומסרה...ומסרוה

Why the term ומסרוה (and they passed it on or down to the אנכה'ג)? It should have either been void of any such descriptive term, as we see in the previous two traditions from Joshua to the Elders and from the Elders to the Prophets, or the משנה should have inserted a similar term with respect to those preceding ones. To stand alone in this fashion is awkward.

We know that there are five generational stages in this משנה, as follows: Moshe = Humility; Joshua = Discipline & Devotion; Elders = Internalization; Prophets = Spiritual awareness; Great Assembly (אנכנה'ג) = Practical Application (the most critical of all). In that final stage, after which there would be no more formal transmission, there is a need for מסורה (tradition) too, not merely Torah (black-letter law). Unfortunately, this attribute is severely lacking today in our general Judea system. And though it may be argued that Mesora is in fact a more abstract or intangible item, nonetheless it's the glue that keeps this whole Jewish thing together, it's the sine qua non of everything Jewish and Torahdic that many, if not most, fail to understand and appreciate. That is exactly the lesson in this משנה and thus the reason for the subtle indication herein by including that term only with respect to the final stage, the stage of "practical application." After all, neither the Elders nor the prophets required it; to them it was self-understood. And though the Men of the Great Assembly themselves didn't require that warning either, they did require the actual passing of it (מסורה) in order to understand and fully appreciate its importance in passing it down to all future generations and that it (מסורה) is an indispensable part of (and perhaps even a prerequisite to) Torah.

As to the question of why this term was necessary with respect to Joshua (ומסרה), I have two answers. First, grammatically it is proper and even required. There's no other way to write the משנה. Why, how would you have written it? *Moshe Kibel Torah Mi'Sinai Li'Yehoshua*? This is a completely unintelligible read. Second, perhaps Moshe at that first level of transmission to Joshua, did in fact need to let someone in the chain know about this מסורה thing and how truly significant it is. (See also later, פרק ג' משנה י'ג מסורת סיג לתורה (tradition is a fence around Torah)).

פ'א מ'ב
על שלשה דברים העולם עומד

עומד bears the numeric value of 120. The number 120 is also the human lifespan, as described in Torah (Genesis). This then may be a hint to the fact that these three critical and integral ideas or attributes (Torah, Prayer and Generosity) are in fact the three key ingredients for long life, for one to assure maximum longevity with health and happiness.

פ'ג מ'ב, ג', ו'
ר' חנינא בן תרדיון...שנים שיושבין...ה'ז מושב לצים שנ'...ובמושב לצים לא ישב

The premise and proof hereof are totally disconnected; it is the quintessential non-sequitur. It reads awkwardly as follows: "Two people that sit together and no words of Torah are exchanged between them, it is a company of scoffers, as it is stated (Psalms 1:1-2), *he does not sit in the company of scoffers.*" How this Psalm is in any way a proof to the premise is beyond me. If the premise were *it is not wise or not good to sit with scoffers*, then this Psalm fits beautifully. But as a proof to the premise in our משנה this verse is wholly implacable and inapplicable.

The very next *Mishna* (3) is equally difficult to fathom. "Rabbi Shimon says: Three who eat at one table and do not speak words of Torah, it is as if they had eaten of sacrifices to the dead [idols], as it is stated (Isaiah 28:8): *Indeed, all tables are full of filthy vomit when there's no mention of God.* But three who eat at one table and speak words of Torah, it is as if they had eaten from the table of God, for it is stated (Ezekiel 41:22): *And he said to me, this is the table that is before God.*" This *Mishna* appears to be a double non-sequitur. In both cases (the proof proffered for three people sitting and not engaging in Torah study that it is in fact as if they had eaten from sacrifices to the dead, and the proof proffered for three people sitting and engaging in Torah study that it is in fact as if they had eaten from the table of God) the premise and proofs thereof simply don't add up. Unlike the problem with the first *Mishna* above, this one's proofs may actually be sound, but they're very general and blanket and appear to be proofs (verses) that would apply to any such table of any number of people, not specifically three (3).

Finally, it is interesting to note, what appears to be, a disagreement between R' Chanina ben Tradyon in *Mishna* "2" and R' Chalafto ben Dosa in *Mishna* "6", in that each invokes a different verse as proof for the notion that when *one* man sits and speaks words of Torah, he is rewarded with God's presence; the former citing a verse from Lamentations, while the latter cites a verse from Exodus.

I could not come up with anything! Perhaps you can. Email me your thoughts and ideas to: editor@davidharppublishers.com.

פ'ג מ'יג
סייגים

Four סייגים are listed in this *Mishna* (Tradition, Tithing, Vows and Silence). But why are the first three listed as they are with the subject that serves as buffer preceding the subject it is in fact buffering, as in מסרת סיג לתורה (tradition is a fence or buffer for Torah) or מעשרות סיג לעשר (tithing is a fence or buffer for wealth), while the last one is in reverse order as in סיג לחכמה שתיקה (a fence or buffer to wisdom is silence)?

A thought: Each of the first three represents or discusses a positive item or an action, whereas the final one is about inaction, a negative. Thus the sages preferred not to begin an expression or idea with a negative or certainly term of inaction, not only because it's simply not a good idea to do so (a lesson we must and should all heed), but also because in this context it might not be grammatically proper either.

פ׳ד מ׳יג
ג כתרים

Though the *Mishna* enumerates four crowns, it begins by stating that there are "three" crowns. There's an interesting subtlty in the word עולה of וכתר שם טוב עולה על גביהן (and the crown of a good name surpasses them all). עולה בגימט׳ 111. Three "1s"; one per preceding crown. This final one is not part of the count because it is above, it surpasses, it is עולה, it supersedes all three, or 1+1+1.

פ׳ד מ׳כב
על כרחך

Merely an interesting and eye-opening observation, and in many ways an observation that can be quite comforting to those who are grieving for the loss of a loved one.

See in this *Mishna* the number of expressions used to indicate the reluctance to be born or created or to live, and the number used to indicate the reluctance to die. The reluctance to live is far greater than the reluctance to die (by a margin of 3:1).

פ'ה מ'ה
עשרה נסים – כפי ששמעתי מר' אלי מאירפלד

Even though the *Mishna* begins with עשרה נסים (ten miracles occurred in the Temple), only eight appear to apply to the Temple proper; the final two apply to Jerusalem – how then do we reconcile this mathematical error?

Rabbi Meirfeld related that in fact only eight, not ten, miracles apply to the Jerusalem Temple, and that there's another *Beraita* elsewhere that relates two distinct Jerusalem miracles. For practical and expedient purposes, Rabbi Judah Prince, editor and redactor of the *Mishna* decided to combine the two (8+2) into one *Mishna*, and because the majority (eight) relates specifically to the Temple, he saw no need to break each one out with separate introductions, relying instead on the logic and common sense of most of us.

I'd like to offer two other possible theories to address this conundrum, as follows:

First, בית המקדש can easily refer (loosely) to Temple *times*, not Temple strictly. And so in fact all the ten miracles referenced here did occur during Temple times only, whether in the Temple proper or even Jerusalem-wide. Hence, do not interpret בביהמ'ק literally "in" the Temple; rather "in Temple times."

Second, we may as well interpret the words עשרה נסים נעשו לאבותינו בביהמ'ק as "Ten miracles were performed for our ancestor *with* the Temple". A Hebrew letter ב serves two grammatical functions or definitions: (1) In; (2) With. Thus, *with* the ביהמ'ק, i.e. in זכות of..., these ten miracles were possible. In other words, the ביהמ'ק (Temple) served as impetus or catalyst therefor.

פ׳ה מ׳ו
ואף צבת בצבת עשוי׳

This *Mishna* discusses ten items that were created Friday at twilight. The last in the list is a צבת (tongs). Oddly though with respect to this specific item only the *Mishna* feels the need of explaining the 'why': Because tongs are made with tongs, whereas it does not do so with all the preceding ones, why or why not? Furthermore, how is this even a reason (for an item to have been created Friday evening at twilight)? Seems as relevant as the price of rice in China(?).

I've wracked my brain on this problem for a long time and came up empty-handed. Perhaps you, my reader, can offer sum and semblance. I welcome same. Email to: Editor@davidharppublishers.com.

פ׳ה מכ׳א
בן חמש שנים...בן שמונים לגבורה
OBSERVATIONAL

Did it ever dawn on you a profound awkwardness in the *Mishna*? Let's review: בן ששים לזקנה, בן שבעים לשיבה, בן שמונים לגבורה (sixty is the age of maturity or elderly; seventy is the age of ripe old age; eighty is the age of renewed strength). Isn't that odd? Here man is growing older from fifty to sixty to seventy, and then suddenly at eighty man is infused with a renewed strength? How does the *Mishna* figure? Are we then all Benjamin Buttons?

Now of course we all have cute thoughts and ideas that transform this *Mishna*, or certainly this expression, into a looser or more figurative, than physical or practical, form. I, however, have come up with, what I believe is, a quite original approach that actually fits neatly with the physical and practical interpretation of this *Mishna*.

If one observes actuarial life expectancy tables, one will find that the *Mishna* is actually perfectly on-point. Though I don't have the exact figures, but the life expectancy, in terms of a percentage of one's age, at eighty, is greater than at sixty or seventy. If we are to take the average sixty-year-old, he may get ten years of life expectancy. At seventy, he may get eight years. At eighty, however, he may get ten or even twelve years. In other words, the actuaries figured that once one successfully surpasses the ages during which most Americans (or even most humans across the globe) pass (which appears to be 76-81, depending on male or female), the life expectancy shoots through the roof – a renewed strength, a renewed energy, a renewed boost of life and longevity.

So the next time you hear "Torah's got it all!" know that it does; it even has (or predicted) complex actuarial life expectancy algorithms in a single obscure *mishna*.

אבות ו:ג
קראו ר'ת קראו רבו אלופו ומידעו

SECTION I – (d)

ארמ'ע

ארמע is acronym for the four elements of life (אש, רוח, מים, עפר) (fire, wind, water, earth) that make up all living organisms, specifically "man". As fate would have it ארמע = 311 = איש (man).

והחי יתן אל לבו
Comforting the Bereaved

This verse in קהלת has been commonly understood to mean "The living should take to heart". What does this mean? Most have interpreted this verse to mean that "the living should take *life* to heart"; in other words, cherish life and don't squander it, for it is oh so precious. This is indeed a fine interpretation. I, however, have come up with another possible interpretation as follows:

והחי (and the *living*), יתן אל לבו (give to your heart). What this then means is that many a time following the passing of a loved one, we lose ourselves and are so distraught that we can hardly compose ourselves and continue living, and as a result are unable to continue life for the benefit of those *living*, those who the deceased might have left behind, our loved ones. At times, we are so wrapped up in our little world that we lose focus and don't pay sufficient attention to the greater concerns, those who are still alive and well. And though it is difficult and though we may not judge anyone during such trying times; nonetheless, it is at such times that we ought to apply this פסוק according to this interpretation (take to heart the 'living' spouses, children, parents, siblings, etc.)

טומאה
מבני היקר הב' הת' מנחם מענדל

We are well aware that there are "50" or נ' שערי טומאה (gates or levels or gradations of impurity). We're further advised that the Jews, upon exiting Egyptian bondage, met with the 49th and that a moment later would have triggered level fifty, the point of no return.

How eerily coincidental is it then that the word טמא (impure) contains the numeric value (גימטריא) of "50", and the first two letters of that three-letter word amounting to "49"?

So in essence the א or אלופו של עולם (God) saved us from utter doom and gloom by removing us from Egypt in the nick of time, at the 49 (טמ) level, instead of the 50 (טמא) level, beyond which there is no return.

יחר – ברוגז

It's quite interesting that the two above terms (sharing similar definition) share גימטריא.

יעקב – אליהו

So we're all no doubt familiar with the idea that five times throughout Torah we find the name יעקוב with an extra (unnecessary) "ו", and five times throughout Torah we also find the name אליה with no "ו". The reason for this is because יעקב took אליהו hostage and demanded release of his children (us) from גלות, and that only upon the fulfillment of this condition (אליהו מבשר הגאולה) will Jacob return the "ו" to its rightful owner, אליהו.

The double question, however, is why did יעקב specifically take the letter "ו" hostage, and why only "5" times?

I think I have a theory about this, as follows.

The numeric value of letter "ו" is "6". So we now have two numbers we must address, "5" (times) and "6" (numeric).

We know that the world is 5775 years old and that משיח must arrive by the year 6000 (שית אלפי שנין). Currently, we find ourselves in אלף הששי or the 6th millennium. יעקב was able to steal the "ו" of אליהו for "5" millennia, because he knew ברוה"ק that there would be no redemption for his children, the Jewish

People, during those five thousand years. By the same token יעקב also saw ברוה"ק that in אלף הששי or the 6th millennium, we will be set free, and so he ostensibly releases s'אליהו letter "ו", for he no longer needs to hold it hostage in the אלף הרו, the millennium of משיח (as assured and guaranteed by our prophets and sages).

כי הם חיינו...מבני היקר הב"ם מנחם מענדל

כי הם חיינו וארך ימינו ובהם נהג(ה) בגימטריא תריח (618).

First, תריח spells חירת (freedom). True freedom emanates from making the Torah and mitzvoth your life, and engrossing yourself therein.

Second, it is written that the אבות observed all of Torah, but that for them, of course pre-Sinai, the mitzvoth were ריחת (merely aromatic: spiritual). Here then we have another רמז to this idea.

Third, and finally, if we are to remove the final "ה" of the word נהגה, which is permissible when considering גימטריאות, certainly when that final "ה" is silent as it is here, then we arrive at 613 or תריג (מצות), the entire thrust of this פסוק.

מזל טוב

The term מזל טוב is loosely translated as "Good Luck". However, I'm not certain that this is accurate. Even if it is, there's certainly space for another possibility, as follows:

מזל also happens to be an acronym for זכר ליציאת מצרים (a memoriam to our exodus from Egypt). Thus the whole purpose behind the word מזל is really relating back to that wonderful moment of יצי״מ (the greatest מזל טוב of all) that ultimately enabled all the טוב that followed us, and continues to, as a people and as a nation, both collectively as well as all the many wonderful personal מזל טוב we enjoy and partake in throughout our lives.

נסיון

נסיון (challenge or difficulty) = 176.

The longest *parsha* in Torah contains 176 verses.

The longest chapter of Psalms (and for that matter, the longest chapter in all of תנ״ך), contains 176 verses.

The longest tractate in Talmud as well contains 176 pages.

The persistency and determination it takes to overcome the obstacles or challenges to achieve greatness and success lies in this very lesson of ultimate Torah study, in reaching the pinnacle of accomplishment and satisfaction.

ממשה עד משה – A bit of levity

Upon witnessing an amazing out at first base from right-fielder (משה), as he leaped in air to grab the ball on a bounce, and threw it, as he popped up off the ground, to first baseman (משה) who caught it just in time as he stretched off first base causing him to fall flat on his chest yet jumping up in time to nab the runner, (it's called a 9-3, for those familiar with baseball jargon), I quipped ממשה עד משה לא קם כמשה.

מנין (רמז)

We know there is a difference of opinion as to the primary, if not exclusive, reason or impetus behind מנין. One opinion is to atone for the 10 מרגלים who reported ill of the Land. The other is to atone for the 10 brothers in the sale of יוסף. In each of these stories, there were two innocents. By the sale of יוסף there was of course יוסף, the victim, and there was his brother בנימין who was absent due to his tender age at the time that deprived his attendance and participation. In the מרגלים episode we have two good spies who spoke positively of the Land: יהושע and כלב.

Watch this. By the brothers we have יוסף the good guy – the victim. By the spies we have יהושע, grandson of יוסף. So we got a connection right there. That leaves us with good guy כלב

and good guy בנימין. If we combine these two names we get the words 'כל מנין בי (every Minyan must be with 10).

Furthermore:

מנין = 150. In מספר קטן, therefore, the גימטריא is 15 (1+5 = 6). This is a clear רמז to the popular concept, requirement, or *halacha* of ששה מתפללים (6 *daveners*).

רעיון מדהים בנ'ך עם המושג דקרי-כתיב
Did Michal (בת שאול) Have Children?

שמואל ב, ו:כג
"Therefore Michal the daughter of Saul had no child unto the day of her death."

Versus

שמואל ב, כא:ח
"But the king took the two sons of Rizpah…and the five sons of Michal, the daughter of Saul."

First the commentary explain that שמואל ב, ו:כג does not mean to say that Michal had no children whatsoever; only that from that day forward did Michal not bear any more children. The fact is she had one son, יתרם, prior to the time period the פסוק relates to. It's quite interesting that there's even a hint to this in the פסוק itself, as follows:

The Hebrew word for child(ren) is ילד or ולד (depending on certain grammatical precepts I won't go into here). This פסוק uses the former in its written form. However, an asterisk appears above the word ילד. The asterisk references that although it is *written* ילד, it should be *read* or *pronounced* in the latter form, ולד.

Often in נך (and at times even in Torah) we find these distinctions between קרי (pronounced form) and כתיב (written form). Most times these clues are far beyond our conception or comprehension, but at times we're given a flavor of their significance and brilliance. Here's one such example.

The numeric value of ילד is "44". The numeric value of ולד is "40". The value difference between the two is "4". Thus, the verse is subliminally sending a message confirming the Radak and other commentary in that one of the five (יתרם) was indeed (biologically) Michal's. The remaining *four*, however, were not, and נך clearly knows this and indicates so.

If we take a further look at the commentary on the latter verse, we find that the sons in that verse belonging to Michal were really her sister's, Merav's. מירב died prematurely, and, in her kindness, Michal reared them, and therefore received the credit as if all the children were biologically hers, a common idea throughout Torah. (See Radak).

So we've got one (יתרם) belonging biologically to Michal, plus four (the difference in the numerology) belonging biologically to Michal's sister, Merav = five. So indeed that second verse makes perfect sense and there is no contradiction here. In fact, the king took the two sons of Rizpah "and the *five* sons of Michal," Saul's daughter. (Also see ספורנו on בעצב – בראשית פרק ג פסוק טז (תלדי בנים).

עצו עצה ותפר

("They (the anti-Semites) cop a plan, and God disrupts.")

When 'they' cop a plan, it's obviously trouble for us Jews, and the trouble can persist for a period of time (Holocaust – 6 years) until God finds the need or will to put an end. So while the plan (the עצה) is still afoot it is indeed, as Prophet ירמיהו said, an עת צרה היא ליעקב (a *tzorah* or calamitous time for Jacob/Israel – the Jewish People). The acronym for עת צרה היא is עצה (the Jew-haters' nefarious plan).

My dear Bar Mitzvah, Mendel, caught me on a rear faux pas. His ever keen memory (kayh) struck back, "The פסוק is not עת צרה..., but rather ועת צרה with the additional letter "ו" prefix". He is indeed correct. But here's my response, one that still preserves this wonderful ווארט.

First, עת is still the שורש, and so the ר"ת still remains intact, as many a time this is the case in either ר"ת or even גימטריאות.

Second, if you really want to be a stickler, you may borrow the "ו" of the last letter of the preceding word עצו, and voila! ועת צרה היא....

שבע מצוות דרבנן

We are familiar with the mnemonic for מצוות בני נח as: א = אבר מן החי: ב = ברכת ה׳: ג = גזל: ד = דינין. Thereafter, we have the letters שגע that are an acronym for the remaining three, ש = שפיכת דמים: ג = גילוי עריות: ע = ע"ז.

I got to thinking, however, and found that there is no equivalent mnemonic for the שבע מצוות דרבנן. So here we go: ענבי החף (grapevines of the beach); a classy reference to the מצד"ר, as follows:

ע=עירובין: נ=נרות שבת קדש: ב=ברכת הנהנין: י=ידים (נטילת):
ה=הלל: ח=חנוכה: פ=פורים

Of course you can come up with many other fine acronyms; the combinations and possibilities are virtually limitless, especially when you consider the cheat factor in that, for example, instead of נ for נשק you may interchange for a ש for שבת. Or instead of י for נט"י, you may interchange for a נ, and the like. Therefore, I went further and came up instead with a fitting פסוק to serve as mnemonic (and though not perfect, it's certainly close), as follows: תהילים ל:ח, a Psalm we recite each day in the שחרית:

(ח) יה' ברצונך העמדת להררי עז הסתרת פניך הייתי נבהל

Notice the seven highlighted or **bold** letters in the above verse, including the verse number, (ח).

(ח)=חנוכה: י=ידים (נטילת): ב=ברכת הנהנין: ה=הלל: ע=עירובין:
פ=פורים: נ=נשק

(I still must figure out, though, the purpose for the verse's words: להררי הסתרת פניך הייתי, although the two-word set הסתרת פניך

may represent פורים, for isn't that פורים? Don't we "hide our faces" on Purim? Don't we, on Purim, masquerade?)

תהילים

We know that reciting תהילים (Psalms) is the truest form of redemption for the soul, (and body). Psalms is recited in times of great stress and despair. Redemption in Hebrew is פדיון. פדיון contains the numeric value (גימטריא) of 150, the very number of chapters in Psalms (קן).

SECTION II – (a)

Vignettes – תבלין

בראשית
ויהי מקץ ימים ויבא קין מפרי האדמה –
מהכלי יקר בשם הרא״ם והצרור המור (מדהים!)

The כלי יקר asks, how do we know that קין brought a scrap offering? Who's to say that flax or linen (פשתן) is not a respectable offering to God? Perhaps one may argue it's no animal offering like his brother הבל brought, but so what? It should still suffice as a legitimate קרבן, why not?

He answers this question absolutely amazingly, as follows: If you spell out the word קרבן in its minutia here's what you get: קוף ריש בית נון. What do those final letters of the word קרבן spell? You got it – פשתן. In other words, says, the Great כלי יקר, Cain didn't merely not offer an animal sacrifice like his brother, and he didn't merely bring something of slightly lesser value but still sufficient. Rather he brought the scraps, the very ends, and the very last of even the פשתן. That was the problem, that was קין'ס peccadillo and that is why God turned away and paid no heed to him or his קרבן.

בראשית
שעטנז – חזקוני ד: ב-ד

חזקוני explains, according to logic, how the מצוה of שעטנז (the prohibition against wearing clothing that are a linen (cotton) and wool hybrid).

חזקוני asks what is the first recorded murder in Torah? It is of course the worst kind, brother on brother, קין והבל. How did this come about? קין brought an offering of "flax (linen)", while his brother הבל brought a sheep offering ("wool"). In other words, says חזקוני, last time "wool" and "linen" mixed, it caused utter destruction and devastation. We do not wish to repeat that.

לך לך
אמרי נא אחתי את
מאת שעורי הר' י' אמסל שליטא (חבצלת השרון)

So ordered אברהם of his wife שרה, upon entering Egypt: "Tell them you're my sister." Why did he so request of his wife Sara? Because the Eyptians were so very פרום when it came to אשת איש that had אברהם not done so, they would have killed him in order to take שרה as their wife or concubine.

The question immediately posed then is, you mean to tell me they were so concerned about אשת איש they would kill so as not

105

to violate, yet they had absolutely no problem with committing a far more egregious crime of murder? It doesn't exactly jibe.

There is a מדרש פליאה (a mysterious and fascinating Midrash) that says: מכאן ששוחטין לחולה בשבת (from here we see that one may slaughter an animal for a terminally ill individual on the Shabbat – generally strictly prohibited –). Ostensibly this Midrash is the only possible answer to our above conundrum, but it makes absolutely no sense – it is simply too esoteric and arcane. How could this Midrash possibly address the question?

The great ר' יונתן אייבשיץ, however, cracked the code in deciphering this Midrash on its own, and simultaneously answered the above complexity – a 2-in-1. Says ריו״א The רן, in שבת, says: שחיטה לחולה בשבת מותר ואפילו את׳׳ל למה זה והלא יותר מעדיף להאכיל אותו נבילה? לא כי בכל כזית נבילה הוא חייב ובשחיטה הוא עובר פעם אחת ותו לא. *(One may slaughter an animal on Shabbat – a generally prohibited act – for a sick[11] individual. And even though one may ask the very reasonable question, why is this permissible? How about if there's a* נבילה *(already dead carcass, though not dead via Halachic slaughter) wouldn't that be a far preferred option, so that one does not desecrate the Shabbat with* שחיטה*? And the answer given is that* שחיטה *is still preferred, because in the case of* שחיטה *one violates a single taboo, whereas in the case of* נבילה *each time the (sick) individual takes a bite, he is transgressing anew).* Likewise, the Egyptians in fact considered murder far less egregious than the violation of אשת איש, because unlike murder where it is a one-time offense, אשת איש is a continuous (grievous) sin each time a man engages in coitus with her.

---

[11] "Sick" does not mean sick with the flu or common cold. Rather in cases like these it indicates a severe illness. Terminal cancer would likely justify such an act.

And so not only did אייבשיץ answer the question of how messed up it appears the Egyptians' moral compass was, but he also addresses quite satisfactorily the מדרש פליאה.

וירא
משעורי ר' יהודה אמסל שליטא

In פרשת וירא the מדרש רבה writes that because the angels did not give God credit for the destruction of סדום, they were punished and exiled from heaven for 138 years. Why 138? What's the significance of this number? The great חבצלת השרון explains: The numeric value of the Hebrew words משחיתים אנחנו (we have destroyed) is 922. Conversely, the numeric value of the Hebrew words משחית י-ה-ו-ה (God destroys), what the angels ought to have said, is 784. 922-784=138.

ויצא
טוב תתי אותה לך מתתי אותה לאיש אחר

(Though I heard this ווארט from my 5th grade Rebbe, nonetheless, I cannot for the life of me locate the source. For years, I believed it was a בעהט, but apparently that's not the case. In any event, it's worth repeating here, and perhaps a reader can direct me to the source).

On its face, what לבן was conveying to his son-in-law יעקב was that "I'd rather give her (referring to his daughter רחל – Jacob's true love) to you, than give her to another man." However, there's an amazing commentary on this verse that interprets it otherwise, in that even in this apparent harmless and even laudatory statement, לבן was still fooling and besmirching יעקב.

תתי = 810

מתתי = 850

לאה = 36

רחל = 238

In light of the above, if we employ the common גימטריא policy of מספר קטן, we get the following:

תתי or $810 = 8+1+0 = 9$

לאה or $36 = 3+6 = 9$

מתתי or $850 = 8+5+0 = 13$

רחל or $238 = 2+3+8 = 13$

In other words, תתי, referring to לאה, I'd rather give to you יעקב. However, מתתי, referring to רחל, I'd rather give to another man, not you. So all along לבן was secretly plotting sinisterly against his nephew and son-in-law יעקב, even when he was "pathologically" trying to appease יעקב and assure him that Rachel was all his.

וישלח
מעבר יבק (מאת הר' נחמן הלוי לוין שליט״א)

מעבר יבק is of course where Jacob encountered a spirit or angel and wrestled with him and ultimately triumphed. In so doing, however, Jacob was injured in the sciatic nerve, an injury that plagued him the remainder of his life. Because of this injury we Jews are forbidden from consuming the גיד הנשה (sciatic nerve, although this really, more loosely, refers to the entire hind quarter of kosher cattle, through which of course the sciatic nerve runs).

Oddly and interestingly enough, if you check your local ancient Israel map of the area, you will notice that מעבר יבק is situated on the border of the portions of Israel belonging to tribes גד and מנשה.

מקץ
ראובן ויהודה (בבנימין)
מהרהג יו'ר חברה קדישא דעטרויט ורב דקהלת הגר'א
הר' ברוך הלוי לוין

The question: Why is is that יעקב was first reluctant to send his baby בנימין with ראובן down to Egypt upon the request of בנימין brother (though no one knew this as of yet), יוסף; yet when יהודה similarly beseeched his father he relented? If at all, it ought to be ראובן the בכור with whom יעקב entrusts his baby (?).

The brilliant answer offered by Rabbi Levine is this: יעקב realized that only his son יהודה truly understood and appreciated what it is like to lose a son – actually two (ער ואונן), in the previous פרשה. He therefore felt safe sending בנימין with יהודה only, not ראובן, reasonably feeling that he could trust בנימין with יהודה over ראובן, and that יהודה will in fact use every resource necessary to ensure his brother's safe return, so that his father doesn't suffer a double loss (as again יעקב is still completely clueless, like the

ויחי
ישימך אלקים כאפרים וכמנשה
מהרה"ג יו"ר חברה קדישא דעטרויט ורב דקהלת הגר"א
הר' ברוך הלוי לוין

Where does this blessing come from? Why did יעקב choose אפרים and מנשה as the prototype?

Because they were the first set of Torah-mentioned brothers who did not fight.

Furthermore, why the preface before the actual blessing of בך יברך ישראל (in *you* shall the Jewish People bless and be blessed)? בך (22) is the number of years יוסף, their father, suffered (in Egypt) – so it's recompense.

My own additions are as follows:

First, בך, or "22", is also the number of years Jacob himself suffered while in גלות (with his father-in-law and brother). In this case then the פסוק should be read, "Even when my children are in גלות they shall be blessed (just as I was)". Second, "22" is also the number of Hebrew alphabets or letters. In other words, בך, in the 22 אותיות התורה (i.e. so long as you – my children – follow the Torah) you shall be blessed.

בשלח
בחר לנו אנשים (שמות יז:ט)

The Midrash says that Amalek chose those men among them who, (the stargazers saw through voodoo and necromancy), were not going to die, to battle the Jews. So the Jews (Moses) countered with selecting men born in the Hebrew month Adar II, for no מזל or zodiac controls that month, as that is technically the 13th month – only 12 zodiacs. (FYI: The author was born in Adar II).

יתרו
נעשה ונשמע מאת ר' לוי גורדון
(In the name of Rabbi Joseph Krinsky OBM)

We find the highly celebrated proclamation of the Jews at the foot of Mt. Sinai, נעשה ונשמע (We shall do and we shall hear), in **24:7** (Exodus).

שמיני - גחון

The חבצלת השרון is rightly dumbfounded about a גמרא קדושין that posits that the reason the letter ו of the word גחון is supersized is because it is the perfect center "letter" of תורה. The חבצלת is thus perplexed how this could be. According to our count, writes the חבצלת, there are 305805 letters in the Torah, which would then mean that the perfect center letter is 152403, but this letter ו is letter 157236, thus making it not at all the perfect center letter.

Therefore, the חבצה״ש brings from the גר״י זילבר that in essence what the גמרא and others mean when they state that this letter ו is perfect center, is not in terms of actual letters in the Torah, but rather so far as "odd" letters in Torah go. That is to say, that there are, according to one opinion, sixteen oddly-shaped letters in Torah, and according to another opinion, thrity-two, and this letter ו is perfectly symmetrical between those that come before her and after her. And he continues to bring his proof from another odd גמרא that says that the words דרש דרש משה are the perfect center "words" in Torah – another apparent fallacy. However, once again, if we count eighty-nine double terms in Torah like נחש ינחש or נח נח or טרף טרף etc., we will indeed find that דרש דרש are the perfectly symmetrical "words" within that pattern.

שמיני
שרץ מטמא?
מאה וחמשים טעמי תורה לפי רבינא
כפי ששמעתי מרבי אלופי ומידעי ר' יהודה אמסל שליט'א

רבינא writes in the גמרא that it is unfathomable that a שרץ is מטמא. He says, "There are 150 Torah reasons (טעמי תורה) why a שרץ ought not to be מטמא (a spiritually-unclean carrier that can pass on its uncleanliness to another)."

For years, scholars have been attempting to make sense of רבינא protest, but could not. After all, seems highly improbable that רבינא actually means that there are "150" Torah reasons a שרץ ought not be מטמא, and so this conundrum perpetuated unanswered for 1200 years.

Then in about 1725, the ויילנא גאון cracked the code, as follows.

The ויילנא גאון posited: One should not read "150 טעמי תורה" literally as I've been translating it heretofore (Torah reasons). Rather, רבינא meant the other (far less popular) definition of טעמי תורה. טעמי may double as "Torah music notes (or טראפ)".

So what now, right? Well "150" refers not to the number as much as it refers to its Torah transcription in words: מאה באמה וחמשים באמה (*one hundred* cubits by *fifty* cubits) when Torah discusses the מדות המשכן. If we take a close look at the musical notes on these words (150) we find the following: קדמא ואזלא מנח רביעי[12]. Translating these words, we get the following: "Previously

---

[12] The actual notes or images are fairly, though not completely, irrelevant. If you, however, wish to see these, pick up your local Pentateuch and go to Exodus, to the portion of Terumah.

[they] went [or walked – upright] [now, they] lie on [their] bellies or stomachs [or crawl]." Which species previously walked upright and now lie on their stomachs? Correct, the snake (reptile). And so finally, says the great Gaon, it is an argumentum-a-fortiori (קל וחומר), as follows: "If a snake that though has the power to inflict death (through its venom), nonetheless cannot (*halachically*) itself infect or affect טומאת מת, a שרץ that has no such inflicting might or prowess (for it lacks the venom to kill), it itself should inflict טומאה? Makes no sense.

"This," says the Gaon, "is what רבינא meant."

(I find this so fascinating and original that I'm not capable of knowing where to begin in my awe of the Great גאון)

אלה מועדי
כמו ששמעתי מידידי ורבי ר' נחמן הלוי לוין שליטא

The Talmud writes that the word אותם in the verse אלה מועדי אשר תקראו אותם (These are the appointed times that they call them...) ought to be read as אתם (*you*, plural). What this means is that which the Jews or the earthly Jewish rabbinic courts call or establish as the holidays, אפילו שוגגין אפילו מזידין (even if they've erred unintentionally or even intentionally) is firmly established as such, no questions asked. In other words, they (the Jewish People) are boss when it comes to establishing the times and dates of year on which the holidays are to be observed.

R' Joel of Satmar and or Rav Kuk offer an amazing simile via argument-a-fortiori, as follows:

If אותם מלא (with the "ו") can be reduced to merely אתם and therefore be permitted the leap into the interpretation of אפילו שוגגין אפילו מזידין, then where the verse in Torah states clearly

(דברים יד:א) בנים אתם לה' *בנים אתם לה'* (*You* are children of God), without the "ו", we may definitely append the Talmud's spin or למוד of אפילו שוגגין אפילו מזידין (even if we erred or even if we intentionally mess up, we are still God's children; He will never abandon us).

כי תצא
Another amazing ווילנא גאון ווארט as heard from my good חבר and neighbor R' Baruch Loriner

Why in פ' כי תצא when the Torah discusses the laws of פי שנים (double inheritance) a בכר (primogenitor) is entitled to, does it spell בכר חסר (without the "ו")?

The גרא posits that it is spelled so purposefully to clearly hint to the פי שנים phenomenon. How so? Because the three letters that make up the word בכר are the only three letters in the entire Hebrew alphabet that numerically perfectly "double" their respective predecessor. This is then a clear indication of the idea or concept of פי שנים (double inheritance to the בכר).

(Not only a giant Torah genius, but a master mathematician as well).

כי תבוא
Anecdotal story as retold by my dear חבר R' Levi Gordon

A wealthy but miserly and nasty individual challenged his entire community and all visitors, that anyone who could answer one question would receive a large donation. Heretofore he stumped every city dweller and visitor, and therefore didn't have to write a check to charity in years. One clever visitor though decided to take on this awful fellow. He entered the magnificent home and was seated at a fine mahogany table whereat the miser was seated as well. The miser smiled at him and said, "So you've come to crack the code. Go right ahead, solve the riddle: A word in the Torah with four consecutive קמץ vowels?"

The visitor responded, "Simple. ה-ר-מ-ח-ה.[13]" The miser was astonished and retorted, "Wow! You got it! But keep it to yourself. Don't spread it please." And he proceeded to write a check. The visitor though turned back to the miser and remarked, "I've got one for you: A word in Torah with four consecutive פתח vowels?" The miser said, "That's easy! ב-ק-ד-ח-ת[14]". The visitor returned, "You got it! But keep it to yourself. Don't spread it please."

---

[13] A type bird whose consumption is prohibited; part of kosher dietary laws.

[14] A type of awful disease.

נצבים – מאת חברי ר' עזרא גולדמן הקדוש

In פרשת נצבים, the Torah portion always read on the Shabbat immediately preceding Rosh Ha'Shana, God says: If the Jews don't behave He will destroy them and their land in the same fashion He destroyed סדום ועמורה. We know that in the destruction of סדום there were *five* cities in all; namely, סדום, עמורה, אדמה, צבויים, צער.

In נצבים, however, the Torah only enumerates the first four and omits the final one, צער. Why?

Reb Ezra offered an amazing thought, so very timely with ראש השנה, as follows:

We know that צער proper was the city from which Lot, the only refugee of the entire סדום catastrophe, was saved. If you recall back in פרשת וירא, in which the Torah recounts the סדום saga, we have Abraham negotiating with God (perhaps there are 50 righteous men, 40 righteous men, etc.), pleading on behalf of the inhabitants to spare the city. God would ultimately hear none of it, and destroyed סדום. With respect to Lot and his family from the city of צער, however, there was no negotiating, because in truth Lot deserved no such reprieve, he was not a man worthy of same. His only merit was riding the coattails of his uncle Abraham, and this Hashem heard and therefore spares lives (Lot and family).

The lesson, going into ראש השנה, therefore is that do not believe you are worthy of any 26, reprieve. Don't come to God with a full accounting as if to say, yeah, I was good here and did this nice deed, etc. We come into ראש השנה with the mindset that we are deserving of absolutely nothing; we are worthless. We simply come to you as Lot did in וירא, bereft of any true merit and we beseech Hashem, to "just cut me a break and give me another year, not for anything I've done, but because I am a child of Abraham, Isaac and Jacob, similar to Lot from צער".

Therefore, צער is omitted. It's God's subliminal message to His people, saying, *I'll spare you, but not because of you, but because in fact you are My children, you are the children of My three favorites, Abraham, Isaac and Jacob.*

SECTION II – (b)

אלקי עד שלא נוצרתי – כמו ששמעתי מידידי ורבי ר' נחמן הלוי לוין שליטא[15]

Why not נולדתי or נבראתי? Why such an obscure term as נוצרתי?

Because any of the other terms would indicate a sad reality in that "God, until I was born I wasn't worthy, and now that I have been, I'm still not worthy." That's one heck of a boost to one's self esteem, is it not?

Therefore, the term נוצרתי is used here. נוצרתי has an interesting alliteration. It's got a נצרך or צורך ring to it (meaning "need" or "necessary"). In other words, "God, until I was 'needed', I wasn't worthy. However, now that I'm 'needed', because after all You've created me, if I am not to realize or materialize my full potential and or purpose, then in fact it's as if I was never 'needed' in the first place."

החותך חיים לכל חי (נוסח התפלה ימים נוראים) כפי ששמעתי מדודי היקר הר' ר' ישראל יצחק טננבוים

Why in our high holydays' liturgy do we find the expression החותך חיים (he who "cuts" life?); sounds rather odd when

---

[15] Although the basic premise of this idea is in fact Rav Kook's, I gave it my own spin.

discussing life and sustenance, beseeching the Lord Who "gives" life?

Midrash writes that the angel in charge of livelihood and sustenance is named חתך.

What's further interesting is that the סופי תיבות of the first three words of the seminal verse (in our daily liturgy) referencing פרנסה (livelihood): פותח את ידיך is once again חתך.

Finally, the סופי תיבות of the first three Torah portions following our annual plea to God for sustenance and livelihood (תפלת גשם), the portions of בראשית, נח, לך לך, also spell the word (or name of angel) חתך.

(My personal addition to this ווערטל is that perhaps this is from where we get the term: *slice* of life).

ים של שלמה
הרהג הרהח דר' חיים דוד קאגאן

In the Book of מלכים, there's a description of שלמה המלך pool's dimensions. שלמה המלך (circa 800 BCE, touted as the wisest man of all) writes, "The diameter measured ten אמות, and thus to arrive at its circumference one must multiply this number (ten) by *three*."

An atheist approached ר' יונתן אייבשיץ (circa 1690-1764), and began to mock and deride Judaism. His biggest proof that all of Torah was nonsense and a complete fabrication was this very description of ים של שלמה. He said, "*How dare King Solomon, touted to be the most brilliant of all humans, past, present and future, commit such a mathematical faux pas, and write that if one wishes to arrive at the circumference of his pool, one should merely multiply the given diameter, of ten cubits, by three? One ought to multiply the given diameter by π (pi, or 3.14)."*

This gentleman now figured he had pigeonholed all of Torah and Judaism, and that he had gotten the good rabbi. *I mean after all*, the man thought, *how will the rabbi reconcile this blatantly irrational mathematical error?*

Unfortunately, however, the feeble man once again underestimated the Torah, as it is indeed perfect. And שלמה המלך was brighter than this simpleton could have ever imagined.

ר' יונתן approached the atheist with ספר מלכים in hand, and turned to the page that discusses the Pool's dimensions. Then he asked the *Epikorus* to take a good look at the text.

ר' יונתן pointed out that the Hebrew word שלמה המלך first uses for diameter is קו (which means 'line or direct distance across'). However, when שלמה instructs us to multiply the קו by three in order to reach the circumference, which would result in an even 30 (clearly a mathematical error unbecoming of the King), he uses קוה with the superfluous Hebrew letter ה. Why?

In Torah the rules of קרי (the read text) and כתיב (the written text) are well-established. Many times, therefore, there will be a word with a silent letter (as in the English language). Unlike the English language, however, there's no such thing as a superfluous word or letter in Torah, as each one has a purpose, a place and significant meaning. The etymology of describing how one may arrive at King Solomon's Pool's circumference is no different. קו is spelled with the Hebrew letters ק and ו, and its pronunciation is the same regardless of the way in which it is spelled. The latter קוה *K'siv* (written version) with the three letters, including the silent ה, maintains the similar קרי (read version) as if spelled with only the first two letters, ק and ו. Nonetheless, שלמה appears to require this extra ה in the second קו for כתיב purposes. So the question is **why**?

Rabbi Jonathan therefore related the following:

Let us multiply the קוה, with the extra ה, by three, as שלמה directs us to do if we wish to arrive at the circumference.

But do not simply read the text (and multiply the given *Kav* measurement of 10 x 3). Rather understand the deeper meaning of the text, the significance of the extra ה – Read between the lines.

The Hebrew letter ק has a numeric value of 100. The Hebrew letter ו has a numeric value of six. The Hebrew letter ה has the numeric value of five. This then equals 111. Now we must multiply this by three, as Solomon directs, and we get 333.

But do not stop there, because we must somehow account for the real קו (the properly spelled first קו - diameter). Hence let us take this one step further and divide by 106, by the real, properly spelled, diameter קו.

333/106= 3.14150943396226415094339622641509, or perfect Pi.

"This," Rabbi Jonathan concluded, "is King Solomon's utter brilliance; he knew Pi alright. But how would a simple, lame and very small-minded individual like you know this?"

ירמיהו הנביא
מאת הר' שרגא פייוול מענדלוויץ זצ'ל (תורה ודעת)

R' Shraga Feivel once recounted that he had a מסורה that when ירמיהו הנביא went down to Egypt into גלות, he met and discussed philosophy at length with Plato (The years fit nicely – between בית ראשון ובית שני, when Plato as well resided in Egypt).

כי היינו...(תחנון שני וחמישי)

The simple פשט of the verse כי היינו לעג וקלס בגויים נחשבנו כצאן לטבח יובל is "When we were like a laughing stock by the nations (gentiles), they considered us as sheep to the slaughter." This of course refers to the hell our people have endured, at the hands of the gentiles, for two-thousand years.

A very wise פוילישע רבי restructured and thus reinterpreted this verse as follows: כי היינו (when we merely were, as we are, proud Jews), לעג וקלס בגויים (we were in fact a laughing stock by the nations/gentiles). However, נחשבנו (when we wished to be like them, counted among them, considered as one of them) כצאן לטבח יובל (as sheep to the slaughter were we led).

This interpretation or translation is not only original, novel and fascinating, but it is also sadly spot on, perfectly accurate. See our two-thousand year checkered history and say it's not so. Just look at Germany 1880-1940 with the influx of the השכלה movement, etc., and see what havoc it and they have wreaked upon our people, all in the name of being "equal" with the rest of the world; not to stand out, not to be different. Though it's a difficult pill to swallow, certainly today, the גויים as a rule (with very little exception) don't like us; they don't care for or about us. How much more do they despise us when we slough off our ways, our Torah, our God, and attempt to be their buddy?

In the above vein, I'd like to disclose something that may come off at first as obnoxious, condescending and even sacrilegious, but it must be said. And once you have had an opportunity to digest and absorb it, perhaps you'll agree: My addition to the above פוילישע רבי *vart*.

What do you get when you reverse ה' אחד? What do you get when you twist and turn the One and Only God Almighty (and His Torah and His instructions and wishes)? What do we get, when we, the truly עם בוחר, veer from the beaten path and abandon the ways of our ancestors, and furthermore influence the sure but steady decline and degradation of morality and engage in its depravity (e.g. Supreme Court Justices Ginsburg, Breyer, Kagan)? You get ד-ח-א-ה (or Dachau); also a "first" (an אחד); first Nazi concentration camp!

This idea also reminds me of a story of the great and indefatigable singer/songwriter and music artist (coined *the Rebbele of Jewish Music*), the late R' Shlomo Carlibach.

Carlibach would say that when he would traverse through university campuses, he could immediately tell who were the Jewish students. When asked how so? He would say:

I would approach a Buddhist and inquire, "What are you?" The Buddhist would of course respond without hesitation, "a Buddhist". I would then approach the Muslim and ask, "And what are you?" And the Muslim would proudly respond, "Why, I'm Muslim." Then I'd pose the very same question to the Catholic and the Hindu respectively and I'd receive respective similar answers. Finally I'd approach the Jew and ask, "What are you?" And without skipping so much as a beat, the Jew would proudly respond, "I'm a human being."

The Jew – So afraid of his own shadow, so great a need to be loved by the world, so great a need to please everyone… except himself, his people, his heritage. A sad but true testament to an otherwise truly unique, unprecedented and amazing people.

משל אדיר כפי ששמעתי מהלחן והזמר המפורסם ר אברהם פרידמן

The camel asks its mother: "Why do I have this thick fur?" Mom replies "Because, dear son, we are desert animals, and to shield us from the hot desert sun God has gifted us with this thick hair." Son thinks for a moment and is rather impressed. Then he continues. "Mom, why the thick furrow eyebrows?" Mom, patiently responds, "To shield our eyes from the awful desert sand and sand storms." Son contemplates for another moment and says to himself, H*mmm, Amazing, Wow!* Son persists, "Why the humps?" Mom, caringly returns, "Because, dear son, we are after all desert creatures and so these humps allow us to store a lot of water so that we may go for days in the hot desert without the need for food or water." Son's now extremely impressed and amazed, and he turns to mom one last time and asks, "So then why mom are we in the Bronx Zoo?"

(I don't believe there is a need to break it down, analyze or analogize; it ought to be self explanatory in each of our lives and in seeking each of our purposes in life).

שכל ומזל
בדיחה כפי ששמעתי מהר' דוד הולנדר ז'ל

Yankel comes to Shul one morning, and his friends congratulate him on winning the Lottery. They ask him: "So you picked the winning number '50', but why? How? What possessed you to pick '50'?" Yankel answered, "Well, it was a combination of שכל and מזל. The שכל part was that my mom always taught me that the number '7' is a superior number, is a special number. So I figured 7x7 must be the best number of all, and so I chose '50'!" The men looked at him quizzically and said, "But wait a minute, Yankel, 7x7 is 49, not 50!" Yankel responded happily, "Exactly, and that's where the מזל comes in – I failed math."

שם הוי'

A fascinating thought I heard from a fine intelligent woman (Mrs. Dr. Brown, Detroit, MI) who attended a lecture I gave in 2014, on my book, *God is Great*. She shared with me that not only is the numeric value of שם הוי' but the same is true in its English counterpart: GOD. If we apply numbers to letters as we do in the Hebrew alphabet, we find the following: G=7; O=15; D=4. Thus 7+15+4=26. Impressive!

תומכי תמימים
(Support T'mimim)

Back in my Yeshiva days (30 years ago), the principal would penalize the boys for either excessive absences or tardiness (and for other matters as well, e.g. petty vandalism). One day, it was my turn as I was tardy several days consecutively. The principal sought to penalize me $20 with the intent of teaching me a lesson so that I would not repeat such lack of decorum. I attempted though to argue and make my case why I should not be penalized. He would hear nothing of it and stuck to his guns, adding, quite aptly and cleverly, "if you refuse to be a תמים, at least be a תומך."

SECTION III – (a)

Lessons & Inspiration – תבלין

**הקורא בסיפורי מעשיות שבתורה הוא
מקושר בח׳ע
(תניא, קונטרס אחרון, ש׳א)**

(He who immerses himself in Torah stories and legends is directly connected with the Divine Wisdom)

אנעים זמירות[16]

The Lubavitcher Rebbe, Rabbi MM Schneerson, OBM, had a custom in the very early years (1955-1970) to teach a new song to his Chassidim each שמח"ת. One such year he chose to teach a song to the lyrics of this liturgical poem. But this time he recounted the following story behind the song:

Many years ago a man walked into a shul, early morning, the day after Yom Kippur. Upon his entry, he noticed a lone fellow at the lectern near the front left of the Shul still in full Yom Kippur regalia (with טלית and קיטל) deeply immersed and absorbed in meditation singing this song to himself. The man approached this singing fellow wishing to inquire as to this odd sight. Upon tapping him on the shoulder, the singer was startled and turned to find the inquirer behind him. The visitor witnessed something he hadn't seen in his entire life. The singer's face was radiant; he seemed to have been awoken from another world or dimension. The singer asked the visitor what day and time it was. The fellow responded that it was the morning after Yom Kippur. The singer could not believe it, he seemed surprised. The visitor asked the fellow, "What's the matter? What happened? Why are you here? Why are you singing this song? Have you been here since yesterday?" The man smiled at the fellow and said,

Have a seat; let me tell you a story.

I was once a very wealthy man. Several years ago, however, I was called upon to bail out a Jew that was incarcerated in debtor's prison by a squire landlord. The sum required to

---

[16] A hymn/poem recited/sung following Shabbat services in most Shuls around the globe, composed by ר' יהודה החסיד in the 13th century.

ransom the Jew was astronomical. I gave my entire fortune of nearly one million dollars. The problem though was that the liberated Jew fell ill and died two weeks later. Several weeks thereafter I had a dream. This fellow Jew's apparition comes to me crying that 'they' will not let him in. That 'they' say he owes a debt, a very large one, that he must make good on it before he's allowed in to Heaven. I responded, "It's okay; I forgive you; I forgive the debt." Upon hearing these words, he was gone. Weeks later though he reappeared in a dream and said, "Although you did forgive my debt and this allowed me to reenter the Pearly Gates, nonetheless in your great זכות of first saving my life from the clutches of earthly hell and then from the clutches of eternal hell, the בד של מעלה would like to repay you, and it's offering you two options in which to receive such recompense: Either the return of your one million dollars. or an out-of-body עוהב experience." I chose the latter. And this, my friend, is what it is, an extension of יו'כ, deeply immersed in God's everlasting grace and embrace in song and poem, a piece of Heaven itself, a song the angels taught me.

EPILOGUE: Rumor has it that the inquiring fellow (or visitor) was the Rebbe himself, but there's no way to confirm same. Even though just the fact that he was the one to recount this heretofore unknown story, should say something about the rumor's veracity. Regardless, this is how we now have this wonderful נגון made famous by MBD and Shira Choir.

בחירות בארץ
(הר' י קמינצקי והר' יואל מסאטמאר)
כפי ששמעתי מהר' יהושע וורנר

In the 1960s and 70s R' Yaacov Kaminetzky of blessed memory issued an edict that it is a מצוה דאורייתא to vote in the Israeli elections. When the Satmar Rov of blessed memory met R' Yaacov on the street, he inquired whether it was true that he in fact issued such an encyclical. R' Kamintezky nodded in the affirmative. The Satmar Rov persisted, "Really? A מצוה דאורייתא? Like מצה on פסח?" Kaminetzky quickly and wittily retorted, "Perhaps more like [17]מרור".

בטוח חיים[18]

Someone once asked the late Lubavitch Rebbe, Rabbi MM Schneerson, of blessed memory, whether it is true that purchasing life insurance is a סגולה for longevity? The Rebbe

---

[17] There's here a double entendre. First, it's as if to say that you ought to hold your nose and pull the lever - a necessary evil (like the bitter herb). Second, nowadays, מרור is a ספק דאורייתא.

[18] Though I've never checked the authenticity and or veracity of this story, and it is fairly difficult to confirm anyhow, it is nonetheless a good one, and is one that could very well be true.

responded: "I've never heard of that, but logically it makes perfect sense. After all, can you imagine the power and impact of the entire John Hancock Financial praying for your good health and long life?"

בין אדם למקום או בין אדם לחבירו (מוסר השכל מדהים!)

Though I'm not sure who the protagonist was, I believe it was ר' שמחה בונם מפשיסחא fondly known as the איד הקדוש (the Holy Jew).

The איד would host many guests at his table, specifically on the holiday of פסח. One year he hosted a non-Chosid at his סדר. When the soup arrived, the man proceeded to crush matzo into his soup (a common Jewish delicacy). The Chassidim at the table were aghast and could not believe their eyes. *How dare*, thought they, *this Jew engage in* [19]געבראקס *at the Rebbe's table!?* The Rebbe quickly caught wind of what was transpiring, and without the slightest hesitation began to crush matzo into his own bowl of soup. Now, of course, the Chassidim were even more astonished, but wouldn't dare question their great Rebbe, and so they continued with the סדר silently. When all the guests had departed and only a few Chassidim remained, they posed the question to their Rebbe: "How is it that the great Rebbe ate געבראקס on פסח?!" The Rebbe responded, "געבראקס (or the prohibition thereof) is only a מנהג (custom); embarrassing

---

[19] For those who are not familiar, געבראקס by Chassidim is considered suspect חמץ; not so with non-Chassidim. Gebroks is any mixture of matzo with water or water-based substances.

a fellow Jew in public, however, is met with fierce Godly punishment of no portion in the hereafter!"

Sometimes we must readjust and recalibrate our moral, מצוה and מנהג compass, and identify priorities accordingly. At times we ought to consider בין אדם לחבירו above and beyond בין אדם למקום. We find that on occasion even God Himself has deferred his honor to that of man's.

בעל התניא (ר' שמואל מונקס)

ר שמואל מונקס was a great and very comedic חסיד of the אלטער רבי (as he is fondly referred to among חבד חסידים) a.k.a. the בעל התניא. The אלטער רבי was extremely fond of ר. שמואל.

When the Rebbe was fleeing the czarist ruffians who were pursuing him for the grave crime of spreading Judaism and teaching ethical monotheism, he ended up running into a home for temporary shelter in the hopes of evading the Russians. As it turns out though, the Rebbe, without realizing, was in the home of his trusted חסיד, the great and indefatigable ר שמואל.

ר שמואל approached his Rebbe, and in a rear moment of sheer contemplation, austerity and pensiveness, began: "Rebbe, if what you've been preaching now for thirty years is real, you have nothing to fear walking out into the open and facing those hooligans because even a bullet couldn't harm you; if, on the other hand, what you've been preaching for the past thirty years is a bunch of hooey and malarkey, then you deserve whatever's coming to you for depriving me and tens of thousands of Jews from luxuriating in all the epicurean and hedonistic vanities the world has to offer."

Upon hearing this brilliant מה נפשך, the Rebbe stood up proudly and marched out into the open air unprotected and unmolested.

בעל התניא (ר' שמואל מונקס)

שמואל מונקס, a חסיד of the רבי ר' שנ"ז ליאדי אלטער, was also the consummate comedian from whom the אלטער רבי derived much נח"ר (pleasure). One late evening ר שמואל was rapping the door of his Rebbe's home and wouldn't let up. After being awoken by the penetrating knocks, the רבי called out, "Who's there?" ר שמואל responded that it is he. The אלטער רבי shot back, "Go away! It's midnight! Everyone's asleep!" ר שמואל, however, would not stop and continued to pound the door. The רבי was incensed but opened the door to inquire as to the urgency of the matter and why ר שמואל felt the need to disturb the Rebbe and his family at this ridiculous hour. שמואל explained that he wanted the רבי to פארברייגנ with him. The Rebbe retorted emphatically, "I will not! And if you don't leave now, I will call my גוי to get rid of you!" Upon hearing these words, ר שמואל broke down and shouted, רבי! מיין גוי איז פיל גרעסער ווי דיינער (Rebbe, my *goy* (obviously slang or vernacular for יצה"ר) is far bigger and stronger than yours). The Rebbe smiled, invited שמואל in and sat down to פארברייגנ.

ר' אהרן בעלזא כפי ששמעתי מהר' יהושע ווהנר

In 1942 when R' Aaron of Belz was fleeing Nazi Europe, he ended up in Budapest for several months (as the Nazis only annexed Hungary much later in the War: 1944). His host showed him the respect he had earned. In particular, though, the host had a 20-year-old son that was extremely caring and tended to the Great Rebbe's every need, want and whim.

One morning in September (אלול), two months into his stay, R' Aaron awoke, nudged his assistant or שמש (that traveled with him) awake and oddly said to him, "געגוג חסד, לאמיר גייען (enough kindness and generosity, let's go)" He blessed the young man in particular with long life, and left in haste.

Fast forward to September 3, 2015 (חי אלול תשעה), exactly 72 (חסד) years from the date of R' Aaron's departure from that Hungarian oasis, and this young man returns his soul to his Maker at the ripe old age of 92.

הגאון מווילנא

The Vilna Gaon once said that the entire Torah and all of creation and all that has been, is, and will be, may be found (is hinted at) in only the first word of the Torah, בראשית. A smart Aleck spoke up and said, "Oh yeah, tell me where the mitzva of something as arcane and amorphous as פדיון הבן (redemption of the first-born son) may be found in the first word of the first portion of the Torah?" The Vilna Gaon responded, "Simple. בראשית is ר"ת for בן *ראשון אחר שלשים יום תפדה*" (The first-born son, after thirty days, shall be redeemed). The smart Aleck was obviously stunned into silence.

הגאון מרגצוב

The Great Gaon of Rogatzov, Rabbi Joseph Rosen, once tested a young man for סמיכה (rabbinic ordination). Upon completing the exam, the Rogatzover told the young man's father he was not going to ordain his son. The father pleaded and clamored, adding, "but my son is an angel!" To which the Gaon quick-wittedly retorted, "Yes, he must be, because קיין מענטש איז ער נישט (he's certainly not a *mentch* (a human being))!"

דקדוק (ללמוד בישיבה)
כפי ששמעתי מאחי הר' ממ פולטר

Approximately, twenty-five years ago a non-Chosid, and one who appeared to be even more than just a non-Chosid, perhaps vehemently opposed to חסידות and especially חסידות חבד, passed the late Lubavitcher Rebbe one Sunday to receive a dollar for צדקה and a ברכה. As he passed, he asked the Rebbe "פארוואס לערנט מען ניסט קיין דקדוק אין אייערע יסיבות?" (Why do they not study **Dik**duk [Hebrew grammar] in Chabad Yeshivoth?). The Rebbe wisely understood this was more than a mere innocent question, and that the man was out more to rib the Rebbe, and thus responded, "דקדוק" (dik*duk*). Embarrased, the man got the hint and moved on.

ר' דוד וויכנין ע'ה
(as heard from my dear nephew, Rabbi Ari Nemes)

The great chosid and Torah scholar, Rabbi D. Vichnin, served for a short while as rabbi of a small and waning shul in Boston, MA. One Yom Kippur eve moments before Kol Nidrei, he was on the street seeking a tenth Jew to complete the Minyan. Suddenly a face that appeared Jewish to him walked by and Rabbi Vichnin asked the man if he would do him the favor of completing the Minyan. The fellow Jew turned to Vichnin and remarked, "Sorry, rabbi, I don't believe in organized religion." To which quick-thinking Vichnin responded, "There's nine men and three women in there, the rabbi's out on the street ten minutes prior to the holiest Jewish moment of the year, Kol Nidrei, fetching a Minyan; does this look 'organized' to you?" The fellow, appreciating Vichnin's quick-wittedness, broke into great laughter and joined the quorum as the tenth.

הקבה מדבר מתוך גרוננו
(as heard from the protagonist, Rabbi L. Groner)

In 1965 a non-Chabad chosid wrote to the Rebbe, Rabbi Menachem Schneerson, OBM, regarding a potential business deal he was seeking to execute. It was a virtual sure-bet, or in today's more common vernacular, a "slam-dunk". He sought more the Rebbe's blessing rather than his advice or opinion. The Rebbe, however, responded in the negative. Upon hearing this, chief secretary, Rabbi Groner, retorted, "But Rebbe, the man is a non-chosid; he is not as prone to follow your advice." The Rebbe said, "Rabbi Groner, that's your issue, you figure out how to break it to him, but that's my final word on the matter."

Rabbi Groner phoned the fellow and said,

Before I offer the Rebbe's response, allow me to tell you a story.

About fifteen years ago I was sent, along with five other בחורים, on a short שליחות internship to Chicago. While there, we were to endeavor in קירוב (outreach) work. However, we also maintained a fairly strict daily study regiment of Talmud, Bible and *Halacha*. One day our נביא teacher (one amazing scholar) walks into class and announces,

I want to tell you guys a story.

About ten years ago my son shared with me his plans for עלי׳. My wife and I were obviously opposed for personal reasons. However, because of my close camaraderie to, and reverence for, חבד, though not a חבד חסיד myself, I wanted to selflessly inquire by the Rebbe [previous, Rabbi Joseph Schneerson] if this was a sound move. I proposed the idea to my son, and my son vehemently and vociferously objected and was irate that I would even attempt such a bold and unnecessary thing.

I was torn. On the one hand I really wanted to know that my son's choice was a good one, was God's Will. The Rebbe's assurance would have given me the mental comfort I sought. On the other, how could I now submit the question to the Rebbe? After all, my son, in no uncertain terms, clearly warned me not to, and, further, that regardless of what the Rebbe would say or advise, he was determined to make עלי, making whatever the Rebbe advised or instructed completely irrelevant to him. After contemplating this dilemma for several days, I decided to proceed and ask the Rebbe for a ברכה for my son and his family, anticipating no issue, but only blessings. Upon receiving the Rebbe's response I found it hard to swallow, let alone eat. The Rebbe's response was a very clear, concise and systematic "NO! Your son should not make עלי!" Now I was in a real quagmire. Here I thought I was doing the right thing against the wishes of my son, and that I'd be able to report to him the great news that the Rebbe blessed his move. This was extremely unexpected and I was disheveled. After much reluctance, however, I related to my son what had happened.

Upon hearing what I'd done and the Rebbe's words, he scolded me and said not only was he not listening to the Rebbe, he wanted nothing more to do with me. Though I understood his castigation and rebuke very well and though I absolutely appreciated his promise never to speak with me again (after all, it was, at least to an extent, my fault), I was more concerned that he would not follow the Rebbe's encyclical. I knew how great the Rebbe was and that if he responded with an emphatic "NO!" nothing good could come of my son's recalcitrant attitude.

My son and his family departed several weeks later. Five days into the trip, the ship suffered serious mechanical failure. The ship capsized, and all 250 on board, including my son and his entire family, drowned.

When I arose from שבעה I paid a trip to New York. During a private audience I asked the Rebbe, "I understand my son's demise; he deserved it. He didn't listen; there was a הקפדה; perfect, no issue. But couldn't you have spared the lives of the other 250? Did they have to go down because of my son?"

The Rebbe looked me in the eyes as tears began to well up in his and said, "Are you kidding me! You think I saw the demise of your son?! You think I saw the demise of the 250 on board that ship?! It's simple. When we Rebbes speak הקבה מדבר מתוך גרוננו (God speaks from inside our throats)! We know nothing, we see nothing, except, as in this case, it is wrong, and it is bad, though we know not why!"

The man on the phone got the hint and did not consummate the business transaction.

EPILOGUE: Several weeks later the Rebbe, while speaking with Rabbi Groner on other matters, inquired as to whatever happened to that non-Chabad fellow Rabbi Groner was concerned would not follow his advice. Rabbi Groner proceeded to relate to the Rebbe the story he related to the man and the resultant reaction. The Rebbe smiled and said to Rabbi Groner, "I owe you a double thank-you. First, that you in fact achieved the stated goal. Second, you shared with me a story of the שווער (my father-in-law) that I hadn't known to date."

השגת גבול כפי ששמעתי מהר' גרשון בעק

A man complained to the Gerer Rebbe[20] that a colleague opened up the very same business directly across the street and that this was destroying his business. The man was so livid that in his histrionics yelled, "I'm going to bury that wicked fellow!" The Gerer Rebbe looked at the man and said, "Wait a minute. You're going to bury that wicked man? Why? You know there's no מצוה to bury רשעים, please don't bury! I know this because it is written that only one fifth of the enslaved Jews actually left Egypt. This would then mean that 4/5 that remained behind perished. It further intimates that 4/5 stayed behind because they were in fact רשעים and didn't deserve liberation. Now if burying רשעים was in fact a מצוה why then did God not command same to the 1/5 survivors?! So we must conclude that there's no מצוה to bury רשעים. Therefore, don't be that hasty, please don't bury him; let's talk about this more."

התקשרות בין רבי וחסיד

פסח ממלאסטוווקע was a חסיד of the third Chabad Rebbe, צמח צדק. He was once fleeing the virulent anti-Semitic blood-hungry

---

[20] The Gerer Rebbes were known to be sharp, witty and quick on their feet.

Cossacks. When he came upon, what could be termed, a dead end in the forest, he spotted a large rock with a sizeable rounded cavity in which he figured he may be able to find temporary refuge. Pesach was also known for his incomparable strength. He lifted the rock up, curled himself up, and gradually lowered the rock upon him, all the while making certain to keep the rock from hitting the ground so that he may get some oxygen while inside of her tight cavernous confines, and that once danger passed, he'd lift the rock from above him and continue to flee to safety. The Cossacks finally caught up with Pesach and located his whereabouts. The five of them, however, attempted to lift the rock, but could not, and so, in great discontent, the head Cossack whacked the rock so fiercely that the rock dropped slightly and somehow made contact with Pesach's head.

As the Cossacks were some distance away and no longer posed a threat, פסח lifted the rock and removed it from on top of him. When he returned home to safety, however, he noticed a buzz or pain in his head and felt a dizzy sensation. As his condition deteriorated he decided to pay a visit to his Rebbe. He was given a private audience during which the Rebbe placed his hands on the head of פסח, and began to cry and mumble several words. When he was done, פסח left feeling completely healed. He had no recurrences until one ערב פסח when suddenly פסח grabbed his head and yelled, "אוי רבי! (Oh! Rebbe!)", and he quickly deteriorated once again and never recovered, passing within the year. Following the פסח holiday, the family learned that at that very ערב פסח moment, the Rebbe, צמח צדק, had passed away.

ואחות לוטן תמנע
(as heard from the protagonist himself)

Rabbi S Kaufman (Detroit, MI) was an older בחור in 1960. As a child, he was struck with Polio, and was therefore mildly handicapped. Though he was not of Chabad extraction, he decided to seek a ברכה for a זיווג הגון from the Lubavitcher Rebbe, Rabbi MM Schneerson. During the יחידות the Rebbe inquired what he did for a living. Kaufman responded that he was a מלמד תשב"ר (a teacher of young Jewish children). The Rebbe asked, "Do you tell the children stories (ספורי חסידים ספורי צדיקים)?" Rabbi Kaufman responded that he did not. The Rebbe pressed on, "Why not?" Kaufman retorted, בטול תורה (wasteful time of Torah study). The Rebbe, seemingly agitated, looked Kaufman stern in the face as he reprimanded him quite emphatically:

בטול תורה? *ואחות לוטן תמנע* איז אויך תורה! זאלסט אנהויבן דערציילן די קינדערלאך ספורים און וועסט נאך מקרב זיין הונדערטע אידישע קינדער לאביהם שבשמים נאכמערער ווי דו וואלסט מיט נאר תורה אליין.

"(Wasting Torah study time?! Are you kidding me?! *ואחות לוטן תמנע* (a seemingly completely irrelevant and superfluous פסוק in Torah) is also genuine Torah! Because after all, *all* of Torah is equally God's Word. You should begin telling stories in class and you will achieve greater success in bringing Jewish children closer to their Father in Heaven than had you strictly taught them Torah)." Then the Rebbe blessed Kaufman with a good שידוך on condition that he asks מחילה of a woman whom he had recently dated for several weeks and called it quits.

EPILOGUE: Kaufman was happily married eighteen months later, and now at age 85 קעלה has raised a beautiful משפחה of

בנים ובני בנים עוסקים בתורה ובמצוות, and established a true דור ישרים מבורך in both biological children as well as thousands of non-biological children, who to this day will sing the praises of Kaufman's superior story-telling abilities that warmed their hearts and inspired their souls more so than any single פסוק or משנה.

חזון איש (עם הרבי ר' ממ שניאורסאהן זצל)

While in private audience with the late Lubavitcher Rebbe, R' M.M. Schneerson, (circa 1960), a woman inquired of the Rebbe whether it is true what the עולם says that the חזון איש has רוה׳ק (Divine Vision)?

The Rebbe responded: א איד וואס ווייקט זיך אין תורה יומם ולילה איז א פלא אז ער האט רוה׳ק "(A Jew who is absolutely and completely submerged and absorbed in the study of Torah by day and by night, is it a wonder that he experiences the power of Divine Vision?)[21]."

---

[21] What's most fascinating about this story is that while the חזון איש was no friend of Chabad, putting it mildly, the Rebbe's impeccable honesty and integrity, nonetheless, went far beyond, and far exceeded, any partisan politics or bias.

החידא[22]

Two brothers, butchers in a town near Baghdad, wished to receive a הכשר (kosher certification) from the great חידא. The חידא refused, remarking about the questionable kosher standards the brothers maintained in their butcher shop as well as the questionable character of the brothers.

While the חידא was once traveling by ship, he ran into these two no-goodniks (no doubt they learned of the חידא travel plans and made it a point to join him). They grabbed the חידא and swung him by his legs overboard threatening to drop him into the cold rough wild sea if he did not give them and their shop a stamp of approval. Upon seeing he had no choice and was on the verge of death, he agreed to sign the kosher certification letter, but he added at the bottom, as was customary in those days, a verse from the Bible. He chose the פסוק in בא that reads: וככה תאכלו אותו מתניכם חגורים נעליכם ברגליכם ומקלכם בידכם – שמות שמות "(so shall you eat the Paschal offering, your loins girded, your shoes on your feet, and your staff in your hand...) (Exodus, Exodus)."

Now though it was very common not only to append a verse from Torah but as well its source, the source the חידא appended was awkward and out of character. It ought to be something like שמות יב:יא (Exodus 12:11). What does שמות שמות (Exodus, Exodus) mean?

This is exactly the question the passersby wanted to know the answer to. Many were rather astonished that the חידא would even lend his name to this food establishment of two very

---

[22] ר חיים יוסף דוד אזולאי (1724-1806)

unscrupulous fellows, and a joint the חידא heretofore resisted doing so. They knew something was amiss.

The scholars of the town carefully dissected the certification letter that hung proudly in the window of the butcher shop when it finally hit them. There was in fact a subliminal message hidden in the odd source שמות שמות.

They said, yes it's true that this verse is from the Book of שמות (Exodus), but why the redundancy? What the חידא was telling all the townsfolk was that not only is this פסוק to be found in שמות, but as well you must refer to the acronym for שמות which, as everyone knows, is שנים מקרא ואחד תרגום (twice Bible and once Onkelos translation). This is the generally accepted manner in which Torah ought to be read or reviewed. They therefore immediately grabbed the nearest אונקלוס on this פסוק and cracked the brilliant חידא code (BTW, the word חידא means "riddle"). אונקלוס translates the words מתניכם חגורים (your loins girded), that immediately follows the words וככה תאכלו אותו (this is how you shall eat it) as *אסורים*, a word that possesses a double entendre. In Aramaic, אונקלוס language, this word in fact means 'girded'; however, in the Hebrew this very same word means 'prohibited'. They got the message.

חפץ חיים
(as heard from his great grandson, Rabbi A Zaks)

When the חפץ חיים turned 70[23] he threw a big birthday party and declared that his formula works: מי האיש החפץ חיים...נצור לשונך מרע ושפתיך מדבר מרמה (the secret to long life is to guard one's tongue from speaking ill of, or gossiping about, one's fellow man).

EPILOGUE: חפץ חיים lived till 95. ודי למבין

טרחא דצבורא

A non-Chasid once posed the very fair question to the late Lubavitcher Rebbe, Rabbi MM Schneerson: How is it that when he davens at the עמוד on his parents' יאהרצייטס, unlike most other rebbes of most other Chassidic dynasties, who take their time and draw out prayer for one to two hours, the Rebbe does a thirty-minute job.

The Rebbe responded "טרחא דצבורא" (*due to the inconvenience of the congregation* does he expedite the service).

---

[23] Considered a long life in his day, because average lifespan back then was only about fifty years.

The man was not impressed and pressed on further, "But wait a minute Rebbe. It doesn't appear you have that problem when you continue ad-infinitem at one of your Chassidic gatherings (פארברריינגגענס), where on many occasions you carry on for 6-7 hours."

The Rebbe responded quite succinctly, "Ah, but my פארברריינגגענס you need not attend."

כל יהודי פנינה
כפי ששמעתי מהר' פסח הכהן קראהן

A man who was very studious, diligent and dedicated to God, תורה and מצות, was one day sitting in שול looking dejected. The rabbi approached the man and inquired into the man's melancholy persona. The man responded that he comes to שול each morning and evening to study the דף יומי, but that he doesn't feel as if it is doing anything or impacting anything. "It appears," continued the man, "that God doesn't need little me studying his תורה and that it's a big world out there with others far greater than I, certainly scholastically. I feel as if there's no point, there's no real תכלית or תועלת and I'm thinking of just throwing in the towel."

The rabbi looked deep into the fellow's eyes and said: "My dear friend, listen very carefully to the story I will now tell.

It was summer 1955 and Mr. Arturo Toscanini[24] was ninety years old, and a great classical concert was to

---
[24] A world-class classical music composer and conductor, renowned for his intensity, his perfectionism, and his ear for orchestral detail and sonority.

take place in Cairo, Egypt, in which Toscanini was ideally to be featured as maestro; however, due to his elderly age and ailing status the difficulty of traveling made his attendance infeasible. Instead, Toscanini's prodigy student would sub for his teacher.

At about the same time, Toscanini was being biographized. Toscanini thus explained to his biographer that because he was going to be busy listening to the Cairo concert on his ham radio that evening, he could not be disturbed and would not be available for interviews, etc. Upon hearing this, the biographer jumped to his feet and exclaimed, "NO! You can't do this! This is exactly the time I wish to observe the master at his skill, in his native setting!" Toscanini continued to object, saying he could not afford any disturbances or disruptions whatsoever, and that he must give all his focus to his prodigy student just this one evening. The biographer though would not relent and kept on persisting, promising he would not say a word, but that he would merely sit in the corner of the room and observe. Toscanini warned him that he may be sitting there for two hours. The biographer smiled and said, "No problem – four is better".

The biographer observes 30 minutes, 60 minutes, 90 minutes without so much as a sound. Thereafter, Toscanini switches off the radio and sits for a few moments entranced. He then turns to the biographer and smiles and says, "You've done well, thank you". The biographer then returns, "and how did your prodigy do?" Toscanini responded, "It was good, but not perfect." The biographer was stunned; he thought it was outstanding. Toscanini continued, "It was a 120-man orchestra, of which 20 should have been violinists, but one was absent." The biographer looked at Toscanini and said, "What? Really? 120-piece orchestra which should have included 20 violinists and you could tell one was missing? From a ham radio no less?" The biographer wanted to go on mocking Toscanini but then caught himself and stopped short, recalling that he was only permitted entry that night on his incessant prodding and at the mercy of his host. Besides, thought he, being as old as Toscanini was, dementia was probably setting in, and so he figured he doesn't know what in the world he's talking about anyhow, so why argue the point.

The very next day the biographer decided to phone Cairo and inquire. He was jaw-dropped, stunned and speechless when the person on the other side of the phone said, "Yes sir, there was to be a 120-piece orchestra, but one violinist called in sick right before the concert."

The biographer ran to Toscanini and said, "My apologies sir. When you told me last night that one violinist was absent I thought you had lost it. I asked myself how is it humanly possible to notice, more so via ham radio, that out of a 120-piece orchestral ensemble, one mere violinist, is absent? So I called Cairo to confirm. How can you tell?!"

Toscanini smiled at the fellow and said, "Dear sir, it's none of your business...No, I mean seriously, it's none of your business. You see music is not your business, it's not your life, never has been, never will be. I, on the other hand, have lived, slept, ate and drank music and musical arrangements and instruments for better then eighty years; it's my business, it's my life. Of course to you and to the overwhelming majority of the world it would make no difference even if five or ten violins, or any instrument for that matter, were missing. But to me, every instrument and every musician counts. I can tell when even one is off or missing, and it's just not the same as when they're all there playing beautiful harmonious and euphonically pleasing music that soothes and serenades. Only then is it truly perfect, is it truly complete."

My dear friend, closed the rabbi, it is true that to me it makes no difference as to what you do or how you do it, nor for that matter what you learn or how you learn it. I may not need another גמרא בלאט from you. But to the Toscanini of the world, הקבה himself, it makes all the difference, and it just aint the same when even *one* is absent.

EPILOGUE: The man tragically passed away several months later after losing his battle to *the* disease. And while sitting at his funeral, the rabbi suddenly hears the man's son closing his father's eulogy with these words: "And with his dying breath, my father left me with these words: 'Don't ever forget, son, that you are a musician in the greatest orchestra, playing on the grandest stage, for the best Conductor of the world.'"

And as two teardrops made their way down the rabbi's face, he smiled.

לוי' של הרבי הריי'צ כפי ששמעתי מהר' יהושע וורנר

The previous Lubavitcher Rebbe's son-in-law and successor, Rabbi Menachem Schneerson of blessed memory, issued an edict to his Chassidim that anyone who had not immersed in מקוה (ritual bathing which purpose is to spiritually cleanse) that morning should not touch his father-in-law's casket at the funeral procession.

A clean-shaven man of about 30 years of age, clearly not a Chabad Chosid, reached out over the mass crowd gathered at the funeral (in 1950) to touch Rabbi Joseph's casket. He was immediately reprimanded and the Chasidim began to shout and admonish him according to the dictates of the (soon-to-be) Rebbe, Rabbi Menachem. The Rebbe, however, was not perturbed, because he noticed something nobody else did. As the man reached out to touch the holy casket, his sleeve pulled up his arm and revealed a tattooed number. Upon seeing this, the Rebbe motioned to his Chassidim to stand down and not to obstruct the man's attempts to reach the holy Rebbe's coffin.

The Rebbe remarked to his Chassidim: "It's okay, he's already been to מקוה".

(A THOUGHT: The man could have and should have responded, "You guys want הגעלה (the lighter mode of ritual purification); I've been through לבון (the far more advanced and thorough form of ritual purification."))

(There's an amazingly fascinating post script to this story I just learned of days ago, and from none other than Rabbi Shmuel Irons, Rosh Kollel, Greater Detroit, who while perusing this ספר for הסכמה consideration happened upon this story, and when I soon thereafter met him at Kollel to receive his הסכמה, he shared the following with me:

> I happen to know the individual – his name is Rabbi Shlomo Greenwald; today, a man well into his nineties. He lives in Lakewood, NJ.
>
> The story behind the story is that Greenwald in fact had just emerged from a DP camp. He wasn't just a Holocaust survivor; he was a Death March survivor too. In about 1948 he arrived along with his young daughter, who miraculously survived as well, on the shores of New York. Not only was he severely down-trodden at what had happened to him and his

family, and at what he had endured, but furthermore, acclimating to the US and finding gainful employment was a major challenge for him. He heard about a צדיק living in Brooklyn and decided to pay a visit and seek his blessing and encouragement. He was going to spend שבת י' שבט with the Rebbe.

He made, what was in those days, the long trek from New Jersey to Brooklyn, via public transportation. He was excited by the thought of seeing the Rebbe on Shabbos and then perhaps being granted a private audience Saturday night following Shabbos. Unfortunately, that Shabbos morning at 8 a.m. the Rebbe suffered sudden cardiac arrest and returned his soul to his Maker. The man was noticeably distraught.

He was not returning home, though, until and unless he participated in the Rebbe's funeral that Sunday. At the funeral, he not only reached out to touch the Rebbe's holy casket, but he further wept and shouted toward the Rebbe's casket פרנסה רבי, פרנסה. After he escorted the Rebbe all the way to the cemetery, he made the long trek back home.

While standing on a subway platform in Manhattan awaiting his connection train, he was approached by another Jewish man who inquired as to why he was looking so disheveled. He simply responded: "I need a livelihood". The man hired him on the spot into a position that Greenwald held for fifty years, and in which he thrived and succeeded at financially and otherwise, until his retirement at age 80.

לקוטי תורה
(as heard from Rabbi Joseph I Jacobson)

During a private audience with the late Lubavitcher Rebbe, Rabbi Menachem Schneerson, a non-Hassidic Jew posed the following question to the Rebbe: "Of what need and or benefit is the study of חסידות?"

The Rebbe smiled and responded: "I have studied Kant, Nietzsche, Voltaire, Kierkegaard and others. I have not found any answers to the difficult issues and questions these men raise…except in [25]*לקוטי תורה*."

מגיד ממעזריטש (at his son's wedding)

At the wedding of the Maggid of Mezritch's (1700-1772) son, אברהם המלאך, Reb Nachum of Chernobyl noticed that the Maggid was withdrawn. He figured it was likely due to the Maggid's great financial hardship, specifically in marrying off his son. Reb Nochum approached the Maggid and slipped him a very valuable gold coin. The Maggid was overcome by great excitement and emotion and exclaimed to Reb Nachum, "Because of this

---

[25] לקוטי תורה is the Great Compendium and Watershed Book of Chabad חסידים and חסידות, primarily discussing such abstract and esoteric ideas like God, Godliness, life, purpose, etc.

wonderful deed you have performed today, I bless you with the following: There is a yet-to-be-born holy soul that's been groomed and polished for hundreds of years. That soul shall come down into your wife and into your lives within the year". Upon hearing this, R' Aaron Karlin, another one of the prominent guests at the wedding, and from the foremost close friends and confidants of the Maggid, exclaimed in great exasperation: "But Rebbe, I've been honing and priming that soul for years! It is mine!"

The Maggid responded, "My dear friend Aaron, I promise you that there's on high the equivalent, if not greater, soul in the female version. She will be born to you and your wife within the year, and she will marry the lofty male soul, son of R' Nachum."

One year later the great Reb Motil Chernobyl was born to Reb Nochum and his wife. At about the same time, Reb Aaron's wife as well gave birth to a little girl. Twenty years later the two were married and together established the awesome Chernobyler/Twerski dynasty (one of the most prominent aristocratic Hassidic dynasties and families) that survives and thrives to this day.

ר' ברוך מזבוז ור' לוי יצחק ברדיטשב

Even though a grandson of the BESHT, founder of Hassiduth, ר' ברוך was no friend of חסידים and certainly not of חסידי חב"ד.

One Friday evening, during a get-together, Reb Baruch announced that whoever would recount a negative story about the great Bardichever Rav, ר' לוי"ק, would be blessed with a portion in the hereafter.

A Shabbat visitor wished to speak up and recount an awkward story about ר' לוי"ק but was immediately tacitly reprimanded by the חסידים. Apparently they already understood their Rebbe's odd ways.

During the Shabbat day meal ר' ברוך once again made his offer. This visitor was once again about to speak up when he was once again silenced by Reb Baruch's disciples. Finally, during the waning hours of Shabbat, during שלש סעודות, Reb Baruch repeated his offer. The visitor could not be restrained any longer and blurted out the following story:

> During a recent business trip I passed through the town of Berditchev. I decided to stop at the local synagogue. Upon entering, I noticed a man standing alone at the front of the synagogue, praying. I stood at the door for a couple of minutes observing the scene. All of a sudden this lone man makes an about face in full *tallit* and *tefillin* regalia and proceeds to walk toward me. Once he reaches me I notice it's none other than ר' לוי'ק himself. He looks me straight in the face and says: *"יוצר משרתים ואשר משרתיו כלם עומדים ברום עולם ומשמיעים ביראה יחד בקול דברי אלקים חיים*... (a part of the daily liturgy); *אבער וואס וועלן מלאכי מיכאל און גבריאל זאגן* (but what will Angels Michael and Gabriel say)?" Firstly, how does ר לוי'ק speak after ברוך שאמר, contrary to *halacha*? Secondly, what in the world did he mean? Did he completely lose it? So there you have it, my nasty little ר לוי'ק story for the night. Where is my *עולם הבא*, my reward?

Reb Baruch turned white, looked at the man sternly and said:

> You fool! You idiot! Do you have any idea what was going on at that very moment ר' לוי'ק accosted you and murmured the words he did? You are so clueless!
>
> While in Berditchev you paid a visit to an inn in which you were attracted to a silver spoon in the restaurant. You quietly slipped the spoon into your pocket, did you not? ר' לוי'ק saw this in one of his many spiritual séances and was attempting to beseech God on your behalf, pleading with Him to spare your life, for up in שמים a terrible decree was issued against you. You fool! Return immediately to Berditchev and ask ר' לוי'ק for a תיקון for your thievery, and

while you're at it, beg him to forgive you for your chutzpah, mocking him, second-guessing him. Once he forgives you, you shall then merit עולם הבא.

מיהו יהודי (הרבי ר' ממ שניאורסאהן זצל)

Rabbi Menachem Gerlitzky is a Chabad chaplain of nursing homes and the aged in New York. Upon his ministering to a gathered crowd in one of his homes he was accosted by an elderly fellow who chastised him and castigated Chabad and its Rebbe. Rabbi Gerlitzky inquired into the discontent of the fellow. The fellow shared with him the fact that years ago this man's daughter was dating a non-Jew, and that he was crestfallen. He decided to pay a visit to the Rebbe and shared with him his story of woe and how much it pains him that his daughter may marry a non-Jew and that his grandchildren, though technically Jewish, wouldn't be raised in that way. The Rebbe 'assured' the man not to worry and that all would work out just fine. "Fast forward to today," continued the fellow, "my daughter married a *shaygetz* and I have *shkotzim* grandchildren…"

Rabbi Gerlitzky was seriously taken aback and not sure what to say or how to comfort the man. After all, the Rebbe didn't offer a 'blessing' as is customary, but rather a הבטחה (an assurance). *How does this happen?* thought Gerlitzky. But then luckily the man continued, "And you know what's worse? What's worse is that nobody, including Chabad, was willing to convert my wife, only the Reform."

Gerlitzky smiled a great big smile and breathed a sigh of relief. In fact the Rebbe's הבטחה, that 'everything would work out just fine, just the way it was intended to', came to perfect fruition. Neither the man's son-in-law nor his daughter were Jewish. (In essence, the Rebbe saved a Jewish man (somewhere out in the big world) from marrying a non-Jewish woman, the man's daughter).

משיח
(eerie story as heard from my brother Mendel in 1985)

In circa 1965, Rabbi Joseph Segal (ha'Levi), ראש כולל צמח צדק, Jerusalem, Israel, had occasion to travel to New York to spend the very festive month of תשרי with the late Lubavitcher Rebbe. Prior to his departure he was summoned into the grand Gerer Rebbe's private chambers. The Rebbe gave Segal an envelope and asked that upon his arrival he deliver it to the Lubavitcher Rebbe and that he also bless the Lubavitch Rebbe in his name.

Upon his arrival in NY, Segal immediately proceeded to 770 Eastern Parkway (Chabad Lubavitch headquarters) and delivered the message and envelope to the Rebbe's secretariat. Rabbi Groner (chief secretary) retorted, "If this is a שליחות from the Gerer Rebbe, you must personally deliver it to the Rebbe." Rabbi Segal was taken aback and not terribly ecstatic about delivering the goods directly to the Rebbe[26], but realized

---

[26] It is customary within Chassidic circles that one not merely visit the Rebbe on a whim, but that before one pays such physical visit it is highly recommended, almost required, that one prepare spiritually and meditate and immerse in a מקוה (a ritual bath) – some even have the custom of fasting the day of. Thereafter, enter the Rebbe's holy

that he had no choice. He entered the Rebbe's private chambers and handed the Rebbe the envelope. Thereafter he murmured, "And the Gerer Rebbe blesses you too". The Rebbe arose from his chair, donned his hat (a common Jewish custom and form of nobility and humility), and exclaimed, "Then bless me; you are a Levite, are you not?". Rabbi Segal was speechless. "Me? I…I…I should bless the Grand Rebbe?!" But the Rebbe had spoken. So he began with the customary "ברכת כהנים" (the Priestly Blessing). The Rebbe replied: "Amen" and thanked him, and Rabbi Segal exited the Rebbe's private study.

Several days later, during the ראש השנה holiday, the Rebbe suddenly turned to several rabbis that were visiting from Israel and exclaimed, "Decree that משיח (the Messiah) must come now!" The rabbis looked at each other, and with humble hubris said to each other and to the Rebbe, "What? Us? Now? Who are we? What are we? We are hardly worth standing within four cubits of your angelic presence. We can't decree anything, let alone the coming of משיח." The Rebbe said nothing further and returned to whatever he was doing as if nothing had happened.

Two weeks later, during the 2nd day of the סוכות holiday, some issue or concern arose at Chabad headquarters (synagogue)[27], and the same Israeli rabbis were debating the issue and attempting to reach a decision. The Rebbe turned from his lectern to the crowd and peered right at the rabbis and announced: עס וועט זיין גוט אבער איר האט דאך אלס געקענט פארשפארן (It'll be okay, but you could have avoided all this nonsense).

---

chambers with great trepidation and take up only so much time of the Rebbe as is absolutely necessary.

[27] There is something unique about the 2nd day of all Jewish holidays; it is something of an anachronism altogether and is only observed in the Diaspora, not inside Israel (where only one day holidays are observed, save for Rosh Ha'Shana). When משיח comes all Jews will be reunited in Israel and of course Israel law will apply across the board and we will all only observed one-day holidays.

Upon his return to Israel, following the conclusion of the holidays, Rabbi Segal was once again summoned into the Gerer Rebbe's chambers. The Rebbe asked him, "So what happened by the Rebbe in NY?" Rabbi Segal was dumbfounded. He was uncertain of what the Rebbe was driving at, so he repeated a dissertation the Rebbe delivered on one of the holidays. The Gerer Rebbe retorted, "No, that's not what I meant – what happened by the Rebbe?" Perplexed, Rabbi Segal repeated another one of the Rebbe's talks. A third time the Gerer Rebbe said, "No, that's not what I'm interested in; tell me what happened". At this point, Segal realized something greater and larger was unfolding here, and he now knew well what the Rebbe was getting at. He proceeded to report to the Rebbe the entire incident, first of his private encounter with the Rebbe and thereafter the ראש השנה episode with the Israeli rabbis, and then again the minor episode with the same rabbis on סוכות.

Now, the Gerer Rebbe turned beat red and began to wail. Segal was conspicuously uncomfortable, but he dear move in the presence of the Rebbe. After about ten minutes of uncontrollable sobbing and shouts of agony, the Rebbe composed himself, turned to Segal and said: עס וועט זיין גוט אבער מיר האבן דאך אלס געקענט פארשפארן.

סבי ר' יודל פולטר

In 1942, when the German Wehrmacht unleashed their terror upon Belgium, my Zeidy knew it was time to go. He packed up his family (wife and three children; the third being my late father Moshe – then only 4-years-old) and fled by foot. After many days of wandering, they arrived at an abandoned train station where an operating train appeared to have stopped. As they approached the train, a bishop suddenly appeared as if out of nowhere and took pity on them and ushered them into the train, the last one bound for neutral Switzerland, and the family lived out the war years there. (Later on, the family learned that the bishop was an apostate Jew named Lifschitz).

This, however, is not the story I wish to relate. The "thrust" story is this:

Upon my Zeidy's arrival into safety in Geneva, Switzerland, he was weeping. My Bubby inquired as to this odd display of emotion. Bubby was perplexed and asked Zeidy whether his tears were tears of joy. My Zeidy responded that they were not; rather, continued my Zeidy, "Today is *Hoshana Rabba*, and I have no *Etrog* on which to recite the blessing."

סיום על מסכת סוכה
(הרבי ר' ממ שניאורסאהן זצל שנת 1978)

The Rebbe had a custom of completing a Talmud tractate on the יאהרצייטס of each of his parents each year. 1975 was no different, and he chose to make a סיום on Tractate סוכה. סוכה closes with the story of מרים בת בלגה an apostate Jewish woman who abandoned her Torah and her People and cohabitated with a Roman general. She so left the beaten path that during the destruction of the ביהמ׳ק she kicked the מזבח and mocked it saying, "You eat alright from this altar; Your people feed You well from here, but look now. When they're being persecuted and tormented, and when Your House is being decimated and desecrated, You are feeble and picayune."

Because of her less than stellar behavior, her posterity (כהנים) were punished and were forced to enter their shift from the backdoor of the ביהמ״ק.

The Rebbe concluded, "I want to be מלמד זכות on מרים בת בלגה as follows: מרים was not mocking, she was rather upset and astonished at what she was witnessing. She was actually crying out to God, yelling at Him to do something and to stop the Roman onslaught."

EPILOGUE: At a פארברײנגען several weeks later, the Rebbe began, "I received a letter from a non-Chabad חסיד in which he laments my recent סיום on סוכה. He writes, 'Rumor has it that during that סיום you in fact succeeded in securing a תקון for the the נשמה of מרים בת בלגה. How if after 2000 years not one of the great צדיקים saw the need or the right to be מליץ יושר on that wicked woman, dare you be מלמד זכות and perhaps assure her soul a תקון?'

I wish to respond to the good man by recounting the following story.

"During the times of the אלטער רבי (my late great-great grandfather), the people were struggling with a דבוק (a spirit). They finally resolved to bring the דבוק to the Rebbe. The Rebbe sat him down and said to the דבוק:

When זכרי' הנביא was prophesying regarding the חורבן ביהמ״ק, a man ran up to him mid-sentence and stabbed זכרי' to death. To date (2000 years) that murderer's נשמה has been a mere גלגול and has found no respite in the hereafter. I wish to be מלמד זכות on that soul in that we know that the only way נביאות may materialize is if the נביא actually speaks the prophecy; if he does not, the נבואה cannot come to fruition. This man did a great service. As is, the חורבן was so terribly awful; can you only imagine had זכרי' הנביא been permitted to conclude his prophesy?!

Upon hearing the story, the דבוק departed. I rest my case".

סלובייציק
(הר' יוסף דוב עם הרבי ר' ממ שניאורסאהן זכרונם צל)

As many of you may know, the late Lubavitcher Rebbe of blessed memory, Rabbi MM Schneerson, and Rabbi JB Soloveiczik, of Yeshiva University fame, were very close friends. They were even חברותא way back in Europe in the 20s and 30s. They attended University of Berlin together, and even after they came to America and established their own dynasties, they kept strong contacts and communication channels open.

On the occasion of the Rebbe's 80th birthday (1982), Rabbi Soloveiczik decided to visit the Rebbe at Chabad HQ in Brooklyn.

When JB entered the בית מדרש wherein thousands of Chasidim were gathered to פארברייננ with their beloved Rebbe, the Rebbe stood up from his chair, something he hadn't done for anyone before or after. JB was only going to stay a few minutes, but ended up staying several hours. Upon his departure, the Rebbe, out of respect, once again arose until JB had exited the בית מדרש.

EPILOGUE: Several days after the incident rumors began to swirl that the Alter Rebbe (The Rav) – the Rebbe being his heir and representative – and the וילנא גאון – JB being his technical heir and representative, had finally made peace. Upon hearing this, the Rebbe quipped[28]: "I'm afraid the בעל התניא and וילנא גאון already made peace in Auschwitz."

---

[28] There is an opinion that it was Rabbi Soloveiczik, not the Rebbe, who so quipped.

עניוות ומענטשליכקייט
הרבי ר' ממ שניאורסאהן זצל

Many years ago a great rabbi or Yeshiva headmaster (ראש ישיבה) of Lithuanian extraction (generally opposed to Chabad Chassiduth) paid a visit to the Lubavitcher Rebbe (for the sole purpose of learning first-hand whether the Rebbe is really that great. He heard a lot about the Rebbe but didn't buy any of it; certainly not the Rebbe's rumored superior scholarship).

He was scheduled for a private audience at midnight (very common). The man was first extremely perturbed by the חוצפה of the Rebbe's secretariat to schedule the audience for a man of his stature at that ridiculously late hour, but he relented.

12 o'clock came around and nothing. 1 o'clock comes around and nothing. He's getting really frustrated now. He runs from the waiting area to the secretary's office and inquires as to the holdup. The secretary assured him that he would be admitted shortly.

The man awaits another hour till 2, then till 3, and now he's ticked, he's had it. He storms the Rebbe's office. Upon opening the door, however, here's what he finds: The Rebbe is sitting in a short-sleeved shirt with a גמרא. An elderly man (with a tattooed number on his arm) is sitting in the seat facing the Rebbe, slouched down sleeping, and the Rebbe brings his index finger to his lips and motions to the irate fellow *shhhh*.

The fellow was both blown-away and satisfied by this classy sight. He required no further proof of the Rebbe's greatness. He calmly closed the door, and made his way out of 770 (Chabad headquarters) with a smile on his face and a spring in his step.

שלום בית

Though I've never checked the authenticity and or veracity of this story, and it is fairly difficult to confirm anyhow, it is nonetheless a good one, and is one that could very well be true.

Someone once asked the late Lubavitcher Rebbe of blessed memory, Rabbi MM Schneerson, whether it is true that folding one's טלית Saturday evening following שבת is a סגולה for שלום בית?

The Rebbe responded: "I'm not sure about that, but I can tell you that helping wash the dishes Saturday night following שבת is certainly a סגולה for שלום בית.

שמירת שבת (מס'נ אמיתי להרבי הרייצ)

When the previous Rebbe first traveled to the United States in 1929 to raise money for his institutions and activities in Russia that were in dire financial straits, he visited not only New York, but Chicago and Detroit as well, among a few other cities. For whatever reason, he arrived in Detroit via the Ann Arbor train station. His famed secretary, Rabbi Chaskel Feigen, received a request from a wealthy Jew in Ann Arbor, Mr. Max Osnath. Osnath made the following wager: "If the great Rebbe would honor me with his graceful presence for a half hour tea time, I will give the Rebbe twenty-five thousand dollar." Now $25,000 in today's money is a very handsome sum; in 1929 it was nearly half a million dollars in today's money. Rabbi Feigen, ecstatic at the offer, ran to the Rebbe and related the offer. The Rebbe smiled and declined. Rabbi Feigen was somewhat taken aback; however, he was at his master's beck and call, and simply returned the Rebbe's declination to Mr. Osnath.

Mr. Osnath was not perturbed and was unrelenting in his pursuits. He therefore raised the ante. "Go back to your Rebbe and make him the following offer: One Hundred Thousand Dollars ($100,000) for a half hour tea rendezvous." Feigen turned white and began to tremble. *This could pay all our debts and solve all our financial problems, and then some*, thought Feigen, and with great alacrity returned to the Rebbe and announced the awesome news! ($100k in 1929 was equivalent to $1.5 million dollars today). The Rebbe again declined. Rabbi Feigen, however, didn't stand down. This time he demanded of the Rebbe to accept the offer. But the Rebbe would not. Feigen pleaded. Rebbe rejected. Finally, Feigen asked the Rebbe, "Why not? Do you realize what kind of money we're talking here?!"

The Rebbe turned to Feigen and said: "You see dear secretary of mine; this is America 1929, where virtually nobody keeps שבת, for hardly anyone can. The few that do, do so at their own peril of livelihood and sustenance – they sacrifice their own wellbeing and that of their families for God and Torah. And, I, who preach the need and great virtues and reward that results from keeping שבת at all costs, am going to spend a half hour of my time with a non שבת observer merely because he has the ability to buy his way with me?! Not in a million years! I will not sell my soul and the souls of my fellow brothers and sisters in arms here in America, those truly special holy Jews; nor will I sell my deepest convictions and beliefs for any money in the world!"

Upon hearing this fascinating and deeply sensitive response, Feigen remained transfixed in awe and adulation of his Rebbe

שריים בחב"ד – הרבי רש"ב

A non-Chabad chosid by the name of ר' יודל עבער paid a visit to the רש"ב. Upon the רש"ב completing his talk or discourse, Rabbi Heber reached out across the table to grab some שריים from the Rebbe's plate (common practice among פוילישע חסידים)[29]. Chabad, however, is opposed to such custom. So the Chasidim therefore looked at him quizzically and with their eyes and facial expressions reprimanded him. R' Yudel retorted in perfect Poilish Yiddish accent: ביי אינז איז שריים מזכה (But by us, *Poilishe*, leftovers of the Rebbe is merit building and sustaining!).

Upon hearing this, the quick-witted רש"ב responded, אונ ביי אונז איז שריים מחייב (And by us, *Chabad*, leftovers of the Rebbe obligates!)

R' Yudel got the message and in fact became a Chabad Chosid, from whom today there are hundreds of fine upstanding descendants.

A CONTEXTUAL or SYNTAXTUAL NOTE: IT MUST BE SAID THAT THIS STORY REALLY WORKS FAR MORE CLASSILY IN THE HEBREW/YIDDISH VERNACULAR, BECAUSE UNLIKE IN THE ENGLISH LANGUAGE WHERE "MERIT BUILDING" AND "OBLIGATION" ARE NOT PERFECT OPPOSITES, AND SO THEY DON'T REALLY SYMMETRICALLY COMPLEMENT EACH OTHER, IN HEBREW THEY ARE AND THEY DO:
זכות is the perfect polar opposite of חיוב (nouns).

---

[29] It is believed to be a good omen or charm to partake of the Rebbe's leftovers.

תוסיו'ט

A wonderful story is told of the holy תוספות יו'ט as follows: After the תוספות (Rabbi Yom Tov Lipmann Heller) passed, his widow remarried. As fate would have it, her new husband's name was also Yom Tov. When she was asked how her marriage was faring, she quick-wittedly responded יו'ט שני לגבי ראשון כחול (the second Yom Tov in comparison to the first is mundane). For those in the know…this is actually a play on a popular expression in *halacha*, in that, in the diaspora, the second day of Yom Tov doesn't compare to the sanctity of the first.

תניא פרק כו – מיגון לשמחה

Sadly one of my congregants[30] lost his eldest son to a seizure at the tender age of 16. One can only imagine how devastating this was for the parents. Ever since then he and his wife were no friends of God, putting it mildly. Time, however, is a healer, and at least for dad, after about ten years of mourning and lamenting, he slowly began to emerge from his depression and despondency. Upon paying a visit to Israel in the mid-90s, he sought, and was awarded, a private audience with the great and

---

[30] Years ago when I served as rabbi of the Elmont Jewish Center in Elmont, NY.

holy saint, the Rebbe of Amchenov[31]. While sitting with the Amchenover, he posed *the* question: "Why did God do this to us?" and he broke down. The Amchenover gently calmed him, offered him a glass of tea, awaited his composure, and once there, lifted the man's chin and looked him in the eye with his gleaming, and said, "I cannot answer that question; no one can. What I can, however, tell you is that it will do your mind and body good to study 'in depth' Chapter 26 of תניא."

EPILOGUE: The man reports that Chapter 26 was in fact life-altering and was the single greatest catalyst in his return as a true בעל תשובה.

תחנון עם הרבי הריי"צ בישיבת תו"ת ווין עסטרייך
(כפי ששמעתי מהר' לוי גורדון)

Upon the previous Rebbe's visit to the Chabad Yeshiva in Vienna, the Rebbe noticed that for some odd reason the ץ'ש did not recite the customary תחנון following the שמו'ע. The Rebbe inquired as to why this was. The ץ'ש explained וייל דער רבי'ס דא (because the Rebbe is present), to which the Rebbe quickly retorted "ווען דער רבי'ס דא זינדיקט מען נישט, תחנון זאגט מען" (when the Rebbe's present; perhaps you ought not sin, but תחנון you most definitely recite).

---

[31] To begin with it's a bit odd how a completely secular Jew even knows of the Rebbe, let alone has any interest in visiting with him and discussing personal matters. Perhaps this is part of the Divine Providence of the entire story.

SECTION III – (b)
בעש'ט

מעין עולם הבא יום שבת מנוחה

Once, during one of the בעש"ט many odd journeys, he was caught up in a severe storm and deluge; so much so that the horse could no longer tug the carriage as the water and mud was just too much. The בעש"ט found himself completely lost in middle of nowhere. It was cold and dark and there wasn't a soul to be found except for the בעל עגלה (the coachman). With no real option, the בעש"ט and his בעל עגלה stepped down off the carriage and began to walk with the help of a little gas lantern. They walked for a long while. They were wet and dirty and tired. Suddenly from a distance behind some heavy brush they noticed a flickering light. They headed in that direction. As they neared the light they noticed it was coming from a shack. They were momentarily relieved. As they came upon the dreary-looking hut, the בעש"ט knocked on the door. At first there was no answer, but after a little while of some hard pounding and shouting, the door opened and a big burly man appeared. The בעש"ט introduced himself and the man showed him and his בעל עגלה in. But as soon as the door slammed shut behind them, the man brutally shoved the בעש"ט while yelling at him, "Go on! Move! I have no time for you! Get inside!" He was brute, loud and frightening. The בעש"ט asked the man, "Can you tell me what day it is?" The man responded, "Why, it's Thursday night, but what difference is it to you?!" The man proceeded to throw the two into a cold menacing room with two floor cots, a toilet and sink, and locked the door behind them.

The בעש"ט was flabbergasted and didn't know what to do. He was, however, most devastated that he had caused the בעל עגלה this morass. They we're both exhausted and fell asleep.

The next morning the two awoke and found food rations near their beds. They completed the morning service and then enjoyed a hearty (not really) breakfast.

After breakfast they began to discuss strategy on how they may escape, but few options existed. They began to pound on the door, but there was no response. Finally, the door opened and the tough guy escorted only the בעל עגלה out, leaving the בעשט behind. The ruffian allowed the בעל עגלה to retrieve his horse and wagon and head back home. The בע'ג though stood his ground and insisted he wasn't leaving without his master. The host bent down slightly from him 6-10, 400 lb., frame, looked the בעל עגלה square in the face as he said, "This is your only chance; go on or your fate is unknown!" Frightened, shaken and teeth-chattering, the בעל עגלה left with a very heavy heart, but decided not to leave completely and abandon his Rebbe; he remained instead within eyeshot of the scary-shack. He found temporary refuge underneath a convenient, neatly designed tree trunk.

Meanwhile inside the home of doom the בעשט wished to welcome the שבת but he didn't hold his breath. He pleaded with his host to allow him to light a couple candles and for some wine or bread for קדוש. The man mocked him and shoved him back into his room and locked the door from the outside. The בעשט wasn't sure what to do or why this was happening to him and whether he'll ever get out of it. He sobbed and fell fast asleep.

As he awoke the next morning he found some food morsels on the floor near the door; he rightly assumed it was breakfast. Though he was hungry he was too pained to eat and so he didn't bother. Instead he tried as best he could to דאוען and recite some תהילים while pleading to God to extricate him from this miserable bondage and hell, especially this being the holy שבת.

Suddenly the door opened and this big auf made his way inside and grabbed the בעשט by the collar and yelled at him to get up off the floor. The בעשט inquired as to where he was going. The ogre was silent and simply escorted the בעשט into his decrepit kitchen and sat him down and forced him to eat and drink something. He permitted the בעש"ט to make קדוש and to wash his hands. The בעש"ט finished his repast quickly and then asked to be excused. The בעש"ט suffered the remainder of שבת in silence.

As soon as evening broke and שבת was over, the בעש"ט heard a clicking at the door. As it was unlatched from the outside, the door creaked open and the faint silhouette of a woman appeared. The בעש"ט couldn't quite make out the figure, nor did he recognize the individual. The woman walked into the room and closer to the בעש"ט and softly asked him to rise. Once he did, she escorted him out of the room into the tiny foyer and stood near a kerosene lantern as the בעש"ט inquired as to where he was and who she was.

The woman began to weep and asked the בעש"ט if he recognized her. The בעש"ט answered an emphatic NO, and then asked the woman, "Who's that man? Where is he? Is he going to come any time soon? I can't be seen, he'll hurt me." The woman, still sobbing, calmed the בעש"ט and advised him he had nothing to worry about, that the man can no longer hurt the בעש"ט. She persisted in her investigatory tactics. "Do you know who I am?" The בעש"ט again says, "No". The woman moved her face very close to the light and told the בעש"ט to get a very good look, but the בעש"ט was stupefied. The woman then began,

> Many years ago when I was only a girl of five I became orphaned from both mom and dad. Your wife was kind enough to serve as foster and did a very fine job; cared for me, loved me and provided for me. One day while in the tub, however, she was brushing my hair, and it was excruciatingly painful, and I cried out, and though you were in the home at the time and must have heard my shrieks, you did nothing to stop it, or to at least inquire. Because of this a great גזירה ensued in the heavenly spheres. On the one hand the home of the בעש"ט gracefully welcomed and coddled a יתומה. On the other hand, however, the בעש"ט is a צדיק and he must be judged כחוט השערה, and therefore it was

determined that you would lose your עוה'ב. Years later my husband, one of the לו צדיקים נסתרים (the 36 clandestine men of great distinction), saw this awful גזירה in one of his many holy epiphonic visions. He could not stand such an awful decree on the great בעשט who saved his wife's life, and so he went to bat for you and argued with the בד של מעלה, but the בד של מעלה would not relent. Finally, they agreed on a compromise as follows: Because מעין עולם הבא יום שבת מנוחה (Shabbos is akin to the hereafter, the glory of Paradise), if I was willing and able to absolutely disturb and destroy an entire שבת of the בעשט, that would suffice and would serve as fair penance for the בעשט and would ultimately absolve him for his lack of thoughtfulness; it would in other words be a perfect trade-off - שבת for עוה'ב.

The בעשט smiled in pleasant surprise, thanked the woman profusely as she sent the בעשט on his way in style, befitting of a man of the בעשט stature, with the finest in food, drink, money, clothing and the finest thoroughbred horses.

קדו'ה

Once, while immersed in one of his many Godly visions or séances, the great בעשט of holy and blessed memory (1698-1760), saw the image of a man who possessed a greater portion in the world to come than he. The בעשט wasn't so much bothered as much as he was terribly curious. When he emerged from his trance he immediately ordered several of his disciples to locate this man, find out who he is, and what he's all about.

The students finally did locate the man but were rather unimpressed. They found him to be a simple and coarse farmer who ate a whole lot. They observed him from a distance for a couple of days, and could just not figure out for the life of them what was so special about this man or why he had earned such a large portion in the world to come. It made absolutely no sense.

After the pupils reported their findings to the בעש, the בעש decided to take a trip down to this man's abode and learn firsthand what his secret was. The בעש, like his students before him, observed the man from a distance, and was, as they were, dumbfounded to find that this man was simply a brute, a bugger, a nobody, who ate like a horse, and was a man of extreme height and weight.

The בעש then decided to approach this man and learn more about him. The man welcomed the בעש and asked what brought the great rabbi to his home. The בעש responded, "I saw in one of my heavenly visions that you're a special man, you're not ordinary."

The man thought the בעש was speaking Chinese. He said, "Me? Great man? Extraordinary? What are you talking about? Are you feeling okay?"

The בעש retorted, "Tell me this, would you? How did you get to be so big?"

"Oh that!" said the man. "That's nothing. I just eat a whole lot."

The בעש did not let go. "Why do you eat so much? Why is it so important for you to be so big and fat?"

The man continued,

> Many years ago, when I was a boy of nine or ten, I was traveling with my father, and bandits fell upon us, stole my father's money and then said they would kill him. They were kind enough to let me go. I watched in horror from a distance how they tied my father to a tree and lit him on fire. My father was so thin and so frail that his body literally crumbled and disintegrated under the fierce flames

within seconds, and turned to nothing but bones. Ever since I witnessed that, I promised myself that I would be the biggest and baddest Jew, so that if ever anything of the like would happen to me, I would not fold like that. Those bandits and all they represented would not get off easy with me. They're not gonna mess with this Jew. I'm gonna put up a fight and it will take me much more than mere seconds to burn up. I'm gonna make sure that if I have to burn, it will take time. It should take time because I for one will not be seen as cheap in the eyes of the *goyim*, as my father was viewed by those hooligans many decades ago. Second, if I'm going down because I'm Jewish, I'm going to make sure that I get my money's worth, I'm going to make sure that I am *mekadesh shem shamayim* to the very last moment, the very last breath, and the longer the merrier. And so I eat; eat like a pig.

Upon hearing the story, the בעשט sat stunned, awed, shocked and speechless; he turned white as if he had just seen a ghost. The man asked the בעשט, "Is there something the matter? Did I say something wrong? What happened? I simply recounted a story. You asked me to explain my height and weight; I explained it. What's the big deal?"

The בעשט looked square in the man's face and said, "I, the great בעשט, have not only not earned your portion in the world to come, I am even ashamed to sit within four cubits of your presence in this world, for I am not deserving of that either. You are too great, too large of a human being, too good a Jew. May God bless you and bestow upon you only goodness, kindness, wealth, health and good cheer all your life. Your share in the world to come is well earned and well deserved."

קפיצת הדרך - שבת

One day the בעשט approached one of his חסידים and said, "I have a mission for you, are you ready?" The חסיד looked at the בעשט quizzically and said, "But רבי I'm a יושב אהל (one who sits and studies Torah all day), what possible mission can you have in mind?" The בעשט responded, "I want you to take the next ship to some far off city, a five-day journey from here." The man turns to the בעשט and says, "What?!" The בעשט insisted that the man, with no further inquiries, answer immediately whether he's ready or not. The man thought for a moment and responded in the affirmative. The בעשט merely gave the man some money for a ticket as well as money to purchase some provisions and bare necessities for his trip, and bade him farewell.

About half way through the trip, a magnificent storm struck and the ship began to rock. All on board were yelling. Pandemonium broke out. The storm intensified. Finally, the ship could no longer endure the wrath of mother-nature and it capsized, tearing up into many pieces. The חסיד recited the customary שמע and וידוי and prepared to die.

The very next morning the חסיד awoke on a slab of ship on some sandy beach, the bright sun beating down on him, the sounds of the sea as it swished up on shore could be faintly heard, but no other sound. He squinted and tried to get accustomed to the light and to the realization that he is alive, that somehow he grabbed on to a piece of ship debris that floated him to this oasis, to this tropical island.

He slowly but surely made his way up the beach and into town. What he found was several tree-lined streets with homes on either side, a strip of shops, a שול and some other municipal buildings. He found it quite strange, however, that there was not a soul to be seen and that not so much as a pin drop could be heard.

He strolled the streets, peeked into houses and buildings, called out to the town, but nothing. He was there alone.

He took the liberty to enter one of the homes and lay down for a nap to quench his exhaustion. When he awoke it was already the following morning, and the town was bustling. People were coming and going, shopping and eating, cavorting and playing, shouting and running, bargaining and cooking, bathing and baking. He stopped a couple of folks to inquire as to what happened or what was going on, but nobody seemed to have much time for him, only to invite him to their home for tonight's Shabbat dinner.

That night he was guest at the rabbi's home, and it was delightful. But whenever he raised the arcane question, he was scuttled and silenced. At the end of Shabbat with the הבדלה service, all the townspeople, including the rabbi, dipped their fingers in the leftover wine still in the plate in which the הבדלה was just extinguished and smeared it over their eyebrows (as is customary), and in an instant were gone – he was once again alone. He could not believe his eyes. He was mystified and terrified.

He ran out of the שול and yelled into the street hoping to get a reply from even one townsman left behind, but nothing. Though he was not want for food or sustenance, nor deprived of sleep, for plenty of bedding and provisions were supplied, he was nonetheless distraught.

Sunday. Monday. Tuesday.

He tried to occupy his time the best he knew how with study of Torah and prayer, but it was little solace as he was distant from home, family and friends.

Then suddenly, Friday morning once again the town was bustling, alive and vibrant. The marketplace was busy with foot traffic and noisy buyers and sellers, and moms were busy with children; while dads were preoccupied with Sabbath preparations. He couldn't get anyone's attention, though.

He was once again invited for Shabbat to many town folks, but he decided to accept the rabbi's invitation. He tried without success to get the answer to his query. Then came הבדלה, and, while daydreaming, missed the moment all the people swiped dabs of wine over their eyes and disappeared in a flash. The man was, more than anything else, dejected.

By now though he was familiar with the routine and began to pick up on the pattern. He awaited the following Friday and when it arrived he made sure to pay close attention, so that nothing floats by him.

This week when הבדלה came around, just as the rabbi was about to apply the wine finger to his brow, the man grabbed the rabbi's hands and prevented him from doing so, while all the civilians did and in fact disappeared. The man then asked the rabbi, "What is going on? What is the deal? Where do you guys go? Wherefrom do you reappear each Friday?"

The rabbi responded, "You have two choices. One, I will crack the mystery for you; however, if you shall choose that option, then you will have to come with us and you will never return to your home or your city, your friends, family or Rebbe. Option Two is that in an instant I send you back to Mezebuz (your town); however, in that case you will of course never know the mystery behind our story. Choose wisely."

Frustrated and torn, the man contemplated his choices. On the one hand he was so curious; on the other he can't merely abscond and never again see his wife, children, friends, and of course his great Rebbe. He finally relented and chose to return home.

The rabbi grabbed a piece of paper, wrote down some stuff (an amulet of sorts, if you will), folded it multiple times and placed it in the palm of the man's hand and closed it in fist-like fashion. The rabbi then instructed the man to concentrate and meditate on certain secret names of God and on certain key

Kabbalistic traditions and philosophies and that if he followed the rabbi's orders, he'd be back home in no time. The rabbi finally instructed and demanded an oath that once the man reached Mezebuz that he would burn the piece of paper he holds in his hand. The rabbi entrusted the man with a match, bade him farewell, swiped his eyebrows and was gone.

The man clenched his fist tightly, closed his eyes and concentrated and meditated on some abstract and esoteric stuff. As he opened his eyes after what appeared to be hours but in reality was only five minutes, he was back in Mezebuz, standing right in front of his home. He could not believe it. He was overjoyed.

He unclenched his fist and it all came back to him; he recalled everything, including his promise to the rabbi. He struck the match and a flame burst forth as he moved the paper toward the fire, but a split second before he could light the paper on fire, a hand from behind him grabbed his, and restrained it from moving any further or from uniting paper with fire. He was distraught. He began to panic. But as he turned around to inquire who was behind him, he noticed it was none other than his Rebbe, the בעשט.

After exchanging niceties, the man apologized but explained that he had made a promise to the rabbi, and that he must complete his end of the bargain. The בעשט calmed him and said, "You've done well my son. It is true that you would have had to keep your promise as it regards anyone else, but not as to me. This was after all my שליחות, was it not? And you have indeed fulfilled it well and flawlessly."

"You mean to tell me," Continued the man, "you knew all about this all along? You knew about my shipwreck and the island, etc.?"

"I did," responded the בעשט, "but it was an extremely important שליחות and I could only send you, my trusted חסיד. Indeed you have the great זכות of furnishing your Rebbe with the key to קפיצת הדרך (shortcutting travel). And now because you have done this great favor for me, I will, in turn, do one for you. I will disclose to you the mystery behind this island and the people who inhabit it.

During the חורבן בית ראשון there was a small caste of Jews who lived at the southeastern outskirts of Israel, and who upon hearing the news of the destruction simply wept. They wept so hard and long that they experienced יציאת נשמה, complete physical departure from this world. Upon their reaching the Pearly Gates a great commotion in heaven ensued. "It is not their time," a voice called out. "So great are they!" bellowed another voice. And another yet called out the famous quote from Isaiah: שמחו את ירושלים וגילו בה כל אהביה שישו אתה משוש כל המתאבלים עליה (Rejoice oh Jerusalem, exult, all her lovers; revel with her in celebration all who mourn her). And so it was decided that this group of Jews get to choose one מצוה near and dear to them that they shall return to earth repeatedly to perform. They unanimously chose the מצוה that most closely resembles the גאולה שלימה (the ultimate redemption and the rebuilding of the Jerusalem Temple): the holy שבת. They have now returned to that remote island each and every Friday afternoon for the past 2500 years and shall continue to so return until the coming of משיח and the building of the third and final ביהמ"ק whence their dreams will fully and finally be realized.

תולדות יי פאלנו
שרשים למעלה וענפים למטה

A wedding between a חסיד and מתנגד was afoot, but not before the decision for מסדר קדושין (marrying rabbi), after lengthy debate, was made in favor of the בעשט over, the leader of the מתנגדים of the day and rabbi of the כלה family, the great תולדות יעקב יוסף.

As the בעשט was later sitting at the reception and פארברייננגינג, his nemesis, the תולדות יעקב יוסף מפאלנו, decided to pay a visit and peeked into one of the hall's windows. He witnessed the בעשט sitting at the head of the table flanked by חסידים and מתנגדים alike, and he heard how the בעשט began:

> You should all know that the תולדות is a great צדיק indeed. He has, however, twice erred. Once was when he met a water-carrier and ordered him to give him water, and upon the man's refusal, cursed him, not realizing that this water carrier was carrying water for the לו צדיקים נסתרים (the 36 clandestine men of great distinction).
>
> Another faux pas was when one תשעה באב he wasn't feeling very well and while sitting alone in the שול a man entered and offered him an apple. The apple was so attractive and succulent that the mouth of the תולדות began to water. The תולדות proceeded to recite פרי העץ, but then he quickly caught himself that it was in fact תשעה באב and threw the apple across the שול. Both apple and man suddenly disappeared.

Listening to this, the תולדות was astonished. *How does the* *בעשט know this?* he thinks to himself. *This is ridiculous!* says he. The בעשט continued:

> Exhausted with what he had just witnessed and endured, the תולדות decided to take a nap. In his slumber, he dreamt that he was roaming freely through his city and, after a while, came upon a lovely lavish apple orchard, something he didn't recall ever seeing or noticing. After examining the breadth and depth of this mammoth and magnificent red apple orchard, the תולדות inquired with one of the caretakers as to whom this orchard belonged. The man responded that it belonged to the תולדות. The תולדות looked at the man quizzically and said, "I am the תולדות and this is not my orchard." The caretaker, however, did not relent and persisted that the תולדות was in fact the owner in fee. And as the תולדות was about to turn away and continue his stroll through town paying no heed or serious attention to this foolish caretaker, the caretaker continued, "תולדות it is yours. You recall that תשעה באב you nearly bit into a luscious red apple, but stopped short of doing so?" The תולדות was now jaw-dropped and speechless. The caretaker continued, "Because you made a פרי העץ but did not eat (though it may have been the right choice as it was after all תשעה באב) your blessing resulted in a ברכה לבטלה (a wasted blessing), and therefore you've created this entire orchard of forbidden fruit; sure they look wonderful, as wonderful as the juicy red apple you were offered by that fellow on that fateful תשעה באב, but looks are deceiving; they're fraught with the most lethal impurities and venom. You must do תשובה. You'll know your תשובה has been accepted when you'll see in a vision שרשים למעלה וענפים למטה (the entire orchards' roots and branches turned upside down)"

The תולדות was startled awake and in a cold sweat, began to shake, and recite the entire Psalms seven times in penance. And though he achieved the decimation of the orchard, and though all that was left of the orchard were tree stumps, nonetheless He has still not solidified a true and complete תקון (soul correction) for that error; he has not achieved as he was instructed by the caretaker, שרשים למעלה וענפים למטה. But if he now wishes for a true and everlasting תקון he should come see me.

Upon hearing these words, the תולדות, as if robotically, marched right on into the wedding hall and up to the בעשט. He fell before him crying and lamenting. The בעשט calmed him, recommended a תקון, and that is how the תולדות ultimately became a חסיד.

EPILOGUE: Although upon the בעשט death, his son צבי took over his father's leadership for a brief period (and of course thereafter the great מגיד), nonetheless, legend has it that on his death bed, the בעשט remarked, איך גיי אף עולם האמת אבער איך לאז אייך איבער יוסל (I'm departing now to the World of Truth – the hereafter; however, I leave you Joseph – the great תולדות)

SECTION III – (c)

Baseball Rebbe

In 1955 a man and his young son entered the late Lubavitcher Rebbe's chambers for a private audience. The Rebbe asked where they had come from. The fellow responded that they were coming from the Dodgers game down the block (Before the Dodgers moved to LA, they played at Ebbet's Field in Crown Heights, Brooklyn). Somewhat surprised, the Rebbe inquired further whether the game was over. The man replied that it was not. The Rebbe pressed on, "Why then did you leave?" The man said because the Dodgers were being blown out in the sixth inning. The Rebbe than asked, "Did Jackie Robinson leave too?" The man, somewhat bewildered at the Rebbe's question, responded, "No, of course not, he's a player!" To which the Rebbe quick-wittedly shot back, "That's right. In life there are players and spectators…Be a player. Don't cut and run when the going gets tough."

Eerie Dates' (Events') Comparisons or Contrastments (reversed or mixed):

1.
1492 (January), the Spanish Inquisition reaches its zenith with the expulsion of Spanish Jewry.

Flip it
1942 (January), the Wannsee Conference whenin Hitler's Final Solution is ratified and implemented.

2.
1096 crusades
Flip it
1906 Dreyfuss Trial (blood libel), France.
Flip it again
1960, Capture of Eichmann, the most notorious murderer of the Jewish People (with the blood of approximately six million Jews on his hands) – He was of course tried, convicted and executed by the Israelis, the only capital punishment ever carried out by the State of Israel in its sixty-eight years.

3.
1948 in Jewish calendar is birth of Abraham, father of the Jews.
1948 in Gregorian calendar is the (technical) birth of the State of Israel.

4.
1649, Chmelniczki Pogroms, in which 250,000 Jews are murdered, (worst Jewish calamity on record until the Holocaust).
Flip it
1946, Nuremberg Trials, in which more than twenty Nazi-war-criminals were tried, convicted and put to death for war crimes and serious crimes against humanity.

Bob Dylan – Zimmerman, (as heard from the protagonist, Rabbi Moshe Feller)

Bob Dylan's native city being Minneapolis (Duluth), MN., he was (still is on occasion) a frequent guest of Chabad of Minnesota and Rabbi M. Feller. One September morning Dylan made his way to the St. Paul Chabad House for שחרית. Following the services, Rabbi Feller escorted him outside to the rear of the Chabad House, a wooded area, and as that early fall wind was blowing, Feller sounded the שופר for Bob, (as is customary to hear the sound of the שופר during the month of אלול). When Rabbi Feller was done, he turned to Bob and said, "Bob, that's the *real* 'blowing in the wind'[32]" Bob grinned and sneered (as he hardly laughs or smiles).

Etymology

There are, I have found, several fascinating etymological likenesses between English and ancient Hebrew or Aramaic,

---

[32] For those of you who don't get the reference, one of Bob's most popular songs that put him on the map is titled "Blowing in the Wind".

lending credence to the fact that much of our modern day English is rooted in ancient Hebrew/Aramaic.

The below "six" obviously sound the same and maintain the same definition as its language counterpart:

ONE:

פרה אדומה may be the source or forerunner for the English word "Paradox" (or "Para" "Dox"). Because the [33] פרה אדומה (Red Heifer) is in fact in and of itself the greatest paradox in Jewish law, and because its pronunciation/sound is virtually that of the English word "Paradox", it stands to reason that there's at least some nexus between the two words/terms.

TWO:
The English word "Alimony" and Hebrew word "אלמנה".

THREE:
The English word "Dilemma" and Aramaic word "דילמא".

FOUR:
The English word "Lack" and Aramaic word "ליכא".

FIVE:
The English word "Regular" and Hebrew word "רגיל".

SIX:
The English word "Sophism" and Hebrew word "ספק".

---

[33] Credit for this one is given to my good friend and teacher, R' Nachman Levine. However, it must also be said that another good friend and teacher, R' Leiby Burnham, strenuously objects.

161

Israel's miraculous survival
(as heard from the protagonist himself, Master Cellist, Marc Moskovitz, Ph.D.)

Marc, a completely secular Jew, was wearing a *kippa* when in 1990 he paid a visit to the *Kotel* (the Western or Wailing Wall in Jerusalem, Israel). While there, he ran into an old childhood friend who had ultimately become a penitent or בעל תשובה. The man inquired of Marc whether he too had returned to his faith. Marc responded in the negative. His buddy continued, "then why the *kippa*?"

Marc began,

About three years ago, I graduated the prestigious West Point Military Academy. While there, I registered to take a class: "Strategy of War". The professor began, "We will be studying strategy of all great wars and conflicts dating back to the Greeks, the Romans, Huns, Vikings, the Hundred Years' War, the Ottomans, and up to the Revolution War, Civil War, Spanish-American War, WWI, WWII, Korean, Vietnam, etc."

I raised my hand, and asked, "Professor, you talk about the greatest wars and conflicts in the history of mankind, and you've even enumerated many or most of these; however, it would appear you've missed to mention some of the greatest skirmishes of all time from which I would think much can be gleaned and learned – the Arab/Israeli Conflict, now fifty-years-old."

The professor looked me in the eye quite sternly and remarked, "We'll talk after class".

Following the conclusion of class, I made my way to Professor's chambers. He welcomed me in with a smile, but as soon as I shut the door behind me, he arose from his chair, grabbed me by the collar and threw me up against the wall, and said:

> Don't you ever embarrass me in public like that again, but between you, me and these four walls, I'll answer your question. We here at West Point have been studying the Arab/Israeli Conflict for as long as it has endured; we've studied every possible angle and avenue; we've examined strategy and procedure and have given ample time to better understand the dynamic and significance thereof. According to all measures and algorithms, Israel should not only not have come into existence to begin with, but should further have long since been swept into the Sea – naturally there's no rhyme or reason to her survival. Therefore, we at West Point have no choice but to conclude that the Country and the People indeed have a Watchful Eye from above overseeing them and their Land; we at West Point are not about to teach God, let alone the God of Israel.

Ever since that incident, I wear a *kippa* 24/7.

Sandy Koufax, Dodgers' Hall of Fame pitcher (as heard from the protagonist, Rabbi Moshe Feller)

In 1965, the LA Dodgers played the Minnesota Twins for the World Series Championship. Because Minnesota maintained the better record throughout the season, it was awarded home-field advantage. The first game that year, as is the case many years, fell on Yom Kippur. Sandy refused to pitch, and the Dodgers lost the game. The following day, Rabbi Moshe Feller, who had just begun his rabbinic position (as Chabad's chief emissary to the state of Minnesota) in St. Paul, paid a visit to Sandy's hotel, and related to the receptionist that he was Sandy's rabbi and that he wished to see him. Of course 1965 was not 2015 and so when a man bearing all the signs of a man of the cloth utters such words, you don't hesitate or second-guess. The receptionist in fact gave Feller Sandy's room number. Rabbi Feller went up to Sandy's suite and knocked on the door. Sandy opened the door and Rabbi Feller introduced himself. Sandy was cordial and invited Feller in. After discussing menial things and sports for about one half hour (Rabbi Feller new his sports, and especially his Minnesota Twins), he asked whether Sandy cared to put on תפילין. At first Sandy was reluctant, but then agreed.

The following morning Rabbi Feller, with great exuberance, related the news to the late Lubavitch Rebbe, Rabbi MM Schneerson, via his secretariat. The Rebbe asked whether the media was present. Rabbi Feller answered in the negative. The Rebbe instructed Rabbi Feller to get the media involved. Now Rabbi Feller was perplexed, but he had no choice but to follow the Rebbe's directive, so he did the following. He called every TV and radio station, as well as all the popular newspapers, in town, and reported to them that he had a big surprise to relate later that evening at the Metro Dome prior to the start of Game 2 of the World Series.

Most of the media were present, and Rabbi Feller announced that LA Dodgers' start pitcher, Sandy Koufax, donned the תפילין yesterday.

EPILOGUE: That day, right in front of the Metro Dome, another 200 Jews donned the תפילין. Needless to say, upon Rabbi Feller's follow-up report to the Rebbe, the Rebbe smiled a great big smile from ear to ear.

Jury in Judaism
US Supreme Court, 2005
(as retold by my friend and teacher הר' נחמן לוין)

Approximately ten years ago, then Chief Justice of the US Supreme Court, William Rehnquist, and Associate Justice Antonin Scalia, were both in attendance at a prestigious Jewish law symposium. During a brief conversation, Rabbi Levine turned to Scalia and posited that, "In Jewish law, if twelve men find the defendant guilty, the defendant walks free (in clear opposition to the American justice system where you specifically need a unanimous jury decision to convict)". Scalia was surprised to learn of this and immediately turned to his colleague, Mr. Rehnquist, and shared this with him. Rehnquist looked back

שבת
Munich Olympics 1972, as related by R' Baruch Levine שליט"א

A young Israeli man wished to compete in the 1972 Olympics. He was one of the world's fastest marathon runners and was going to compete in the Track & Field competition, and by most odd-makers' estimation he was the favorite to take home gold. The problem, however, was that he had, just prior to the 1972 Olympics, become a penitent (he returned to his Heritage, Tradition, God and People), and the Track & Field competitions were scheduled for Saturday, the day of the Jewish Sabbath, on which any such profane exercises are strictly prohibited. He attempted to reason with, and appeal to, the Olympic authorities, but to no avail. Thus he chose "faith" over "fame and fortune", and did not participate in the 1972 Munich Olympics.

EPILOGUE: By now you are no doubt familiar with the *1972 Munich Olympics Israeli Athletes Massacre* which resulted in the murder of all 11 Israeli athletes that competed in the 1972 Olympics. שבת ultimately saved this man's life.

Two interesting and fairly unknown symbol sources:

The name of this symbol is *Caduceus*. There's not much on the origin of this symbol as it relates to the medical field. Wikipedia has its opinions. The most sensible and dominant, however, is to be found in Numbers 21:8. (See חקת – נחש נחשת).

The name of this symbol is *Olive Branch*. We know that this has come to represent the idea of "peace", but wherefrom do we get the leap from 'olive branch' to 'peace'? How does a meaningless olive branch get to represent something as lofty as peace? Well once again straight out of the Torah at Genesis 8:11 (when Noah sent the Dove to test for dryness of land following the Great Deluge, and the Dove returned with an Olive Branch in its beak confirming dryness of land and thus the arresting of God's wrath. It has therefore become synonymous with the ultimate symbol of peace and tranquility, and a sign that indicated permissibility for humans, and all living things or organisms to once again inhabit the earth).

One Perfect Last One

As I close out this wonderful work I leave you with this, a fitting closing.

The slow but steady degradation and troubles and pain first began with a נחש (snake). It all ends with the coming of משיח speedily. Then it'll be so awesome that we will finally realize how two-thsousand years of hell (and to a larger extent, 5780 years of unrelenting and unforgiving and indescribable horror) were all worth it.

To tie it all together in a stunning bow and נעוץ תחלתן בסופן וסופן בתחלתן see how נחש and משיח share the very same גימטריא – numeric value: 358.

TEST YOUR JEWISH/ISRAEL KNOWLEDGE:

FUN GENERAL JEWISH TRIVIA – 55 points: Good. 65 points: Excellent. Otherwise, back to school.

DISCLAIMER: You of course can cheat all you want, but what's the point? You'll only be fooling yourself.

1. Number countries Rambam resided in? Which? (2)
2. Which *Shevet* had most kids? How many? (2)
3. You would find *Hilchot Pesach* in this *Chelek Shulchan Aruch*? (1)
4. Who authored *Gur Aryeh*? (1)
5. R' Chaim Vital's teacher? (2)
6. This commentary on Chumash was authored by R' Shlomo Ephraim? (1)
7. PM of Israel during 6-Day War? (2)
8. Which famous city in Israel is **not** *Eretz Yisroel min ha'Torah*? (1)
9. This famous sefer was authored by R' Bachye Ibn Pakuda? (2)
10. Rambam's b-day? (2)
11. Author of *Megillat Rus*? (2)
12. Author of Book of Samuel? (3)
    a. Prophet Shmuel
    b. Prophet Isaiah
    c. Prophet Nosson
    d. Prophet Gad
13. Parsha covering longest period (over 1000 years)? (1)
14. This man was Kalba Savua's son-in-law? (1)
15. Kohelet author? (1)
16. Longest Talmud Tractate? (1)
17. *Me'or ha'Goleh*? (1)

18. *Haftorat Machar Chodesh* is read when? (1)
19. 30 is the age of _____ in *Gimatria*? (2)
20. This commentary on SA was authored by R' Dovid ben Shmuel ha'Levi? (1)
21. R' Elijah Kramer was also famously known as? (2)
22. R' Yaacov Meir ben Asher wrote this commentary on Chumash? (1)
23. Chana traveled to the *Mishkan* in this city _____ to pray for a son? (1)
24. Jew cleared of blood libel in 1917? (1)
25. Jew cleared of blood libel in 1905? (2)
26. Ramchal? (1)
27. On this RC we recite whole *Hallel*? (1)
28. On this RC we do not recite *Hallel*? (1)
29. Largest chapter in Tanach? (1)
30. He replaced his father Shlomo as King? (2)
31. King Saul's minister of defense? (2)
32. She reported to Yaacov that Joseph still alive? (1)
33. Author of *Kitzur*? (1)
34. Queens Esther's father? (2)
35. Saul's daughter, David's wife? (1)
36. He abdicated his father-in-law? (2)
37. Which of the following least belongs with other, and why? (2)
    a. David & Absalom
    b. David & Solomon
    c. David & Nathan
    d. Solomon & Rehabam
    e. Issac & Jacob
38. The first three Mitzvoth in Torah are: (2)
    a. Positive, Positive, Negative
    b. Positive, Negative, Positive
    c. Negative, Negative, Negative
    d. Negative, Positive, Negative
    e. Positive, Negative, Negative

39. This holiday has no date certain as do the others? (2)
    a. Pesach
    b. Succoth
    c. Shvu'oth
    d. Hanukkah
    e. Purim
    f. Yom Kippur
40. Other than 5 *Megilloth*, another two books of *Nach* that fall into *Ketuvim*? (2)
41. How many days in a fortnight? (2)
42. How many times does the טראפ מרכא כפולה appear in the Torah? (3)
43. As to "42" which סדרות? (4)
44. As to "43" which words? (5)
45. Who's the only Jew a Chabad Rebbe appended the accolade *Yimach Shemo*? (3)
    a. Karl Marx
    b. Moses Mendelsohn
    c. Sigmund Freud
    d. Albert Einstein
    e. Avigdor
    f. Spinoza
46. What is the only "obscure" and rarely-performed מצוה that requires its performance in the presence of three men (דיינים), of which the רמבם disqualifies the men even if *fully* Jewish *halachically*, (i.e. even if born to a Jewish mother - more is required)? (4)
47. Besides *Midbar* (desert), the משכן resided in four cities in Israel before the Jews (שלמה) formally built the בית המקדש. Name the four cities, and in which of those cities did it reside longest and how long was that? (4)
48. Although technically you find three מצוות in the Book of בראשית, we really don't. In other words, the three ostensible מצוות are (1) פרו ורבו (2) מילה (3) גיד הנשה. However, it is not as simple as it appears for the following

reasons. You see, although they seem 'commanded' in בראשית they were nonetheless not performed in בראשית, for the time period בראשית recounts predated Sinai (and thus, the giving of the Torah and its mitzvoth) by thousands of years. There is, however, one מצוה in the book of בראשית that oddly enough is recounted to us, not just as a historical idea or a Godly commandment, but it is retold to us in a way wherein it would appear that they actually observed it back then, pre Torah (this is unique)[34]. Which one? (4)

ANSWER KEY

1. 4 – Spain, Morocco, Israel, Egypt
2. Binyamin, 10
3. Orach Chaim
4. Maharal
5. Ari or Ramak
6. Klei Yakar
7. Levi Eshkol
8. Eilat
9. Chovot hal'vavoth
10. 14 Nissan (Erev Pesach)
11. Prophet Samuel
12. (d) Prophet Gad
13. Bereishit
14. Akiva
15. King Solomon
16. Baba Batra
17. Rabeinu Gershom
18. RC is Sunday

---

[34] Brit Milah may be a close second, but not as cut and dry. (Technically, the "commandment" is later on in *Tazria*).

19. Koach (strength or power)
20. Taz
21. Vilna Gaon
22. Baal ha'Turim
23. Shiloh
24. Mendel Baylis
25. Al Dreyfus
26. R' Moshe Chaim Lutzato
27. Tevet
28. Tishrei
29. 119
30. Rehabam
31. Abner
32. Serah
33. Ganzfried
34. Abichayil
35. Michal
36. King David
37. (c)David & Nathan, the only non father-son pair
38. (a) פרו ורבו, מילה, גיד הנשה
39. (c) Shvu'oth
40. תהילים, איוב, משלי, עזרא, דניאל, ד'ה
41. 14
42. 5
43. תולדות, שמות, שמיני, שלח, מטות
44. לו, תעשה, לא, טוב, לה
45. (b)
46. חליצה – both mom *and* dad of all three men (judges) must be Jewish; mom's Jewishness alone does not qualify (רמבם הל' יבום וחליצה פ'ד ה'ה). [This is the only such instance in all of Torah, where that is the case – i.e. where exclusive matrilineal descent, as is otherwise the case, is not sufficient to qualify the offspring as Jewish (judges)].
47. 4; גלגל, שילה, נב, גבעון; Shiloh – 370 years
48. יבום: פ' וישב עם יהודה ער אונן ושלה

www.ingramcontent.com/pod-product-compliance
Lightning Source LLC
LaVergne TN
LVHW041249080426
835510LV00009B/663